AF600165

Ecclesiastical Sepulture

in the

New Code of Canon Law

A DISSERTATION

*Submitted to the Faculty of Sacred Sciences of the
Catholic University of America
in partial fulfillment of the requirements
for the Degree*

DOCTOR OF CANON LAW

by the

REV. JOHN ANTHONY O'REILLY, S.T.B., J.C.L.
of the Archdiocese of Ottawa

1923

Nihil Obstat.

THOMAS J. SHAHAN, S. T. D.,

Censor Deputatus.

Imprimatur.

MICHAEL J. CURLEY, D. D.,

Archiepiscopus Baltimorensis.

CONTENTS

INTRODUCTION

The human race has had many problems and mysteries to contend with ever since the beginning, and probably the most decisive, yet baffling, is that of death. But a scarce moment and the spark has flickered out to leave a flesh-and-blood body tenantless of spirit and life. The question of disposing of the human body after death has claimed the soul, has occupied a position of concern among all classes and manners of peoples at all times. Their motives for this have been diverse; the cause of such differences may be traced to the varied conceptions of spirituality peculiar to place and period, and to the conflicting opinions on the life after death.

I. Ecclesiastical Sepulture

The reverence, disposition and deposition of the bodies of the faithful departed, Holy Mother Church considers an integral and important feature of our holy religion. Ever solicitous for the spiritual and religious fitness of things, and for the happy association of Heaven with our present existence, the Church, in her codification of regulations and discipline, has in every age given due prominence and attention to the various matters which bear on ecclesiastical sepulture. In the New Code of Canon Law we find a complete "Titulus" devoted to this subject, under which is grouped a number of canons which present an excellent treatise in a highly commendable form.

1. *Order followed in the New Code*

In the scientific order of the New Code, the Third Book consists of five Parts. Part second is subdivided into two Sections and the first of these Sections treats of Sacred Places. The fourth and last Title of this Section is "Titulus XII," on "Ecclesiastical Sepulture."

This Title is composed of three Chapters: (1) concerning cemeteries; (2) concerning the translation of the body to the church, the funeral and burial; and (3) concerning those to whom is granted ecclesiastical sepulture, and those denied. Since the plan of this treatise is to compare and comment on the law of the New Code in comparison with the former legislation, this order used in the New Code will be followed. To some it might seem rather strange that the New Code should allot the chapter on cemeteries and those which treat of ecclesiastical sepulture, under the one title "Ecclesiastical Sepulture" in the section on "Sacred Places." For this is not the traditional form employed in treating of these two subjects. Cemeteries were treated in the chapter on Sacred Places, while the regulations concerning ecclesiastical sepulture were discussed under the general heading or chapter on the Sacramentals.[1] However, since the New Code has placed the two under the one heading of "Ecclesiastical Sepulture," which is a highly suitable arrangement, the same will be followed in this treatise.

2. *Canonical signification*

From the name itself one ordinarily presumes that "Sepulture" refers to the burial of the bodies of the dead; and in the past, this term was often applied to denote the place of burial.[2] "Ecclesiastical Sepulture" however, enjoys a triple signification in the new Canon Law, and in this import will the term be employed throughout this treatise. First, it denotes that place blessed by ecclesiastical authority for the burial of the bodies of the faithful departed. Secondly, it refers to those universal sacred rites prescribed by the Church for the interment of her departed members. Thirdly, it refers to that inalienable right which the Church

---

1 Wernz, "Jus Decretalium," Tom. III. Pars. Secunda, Sect. I, Cap. II, Tit. XVII, No. 4 and Sect. II, Cap. II, Tit. XXXIII.

2 C. 14, C. 13, Q. 2; Reiffenstuel, "Jus Canonicum," Tom. 4; Tit. XXVIII, No. 3.

possesses of complete dominion over the concession or denial of this ordinance.[3]

II. Concerning Cremation

The Church has ever been consistent in reprobation of the practice of cremating the bodies of the dead. This usage is abhorrent to the spirit of Christianity and society, with few exceptions has constantly had a pronounced aversion for it.[4] True, there have been certain types of pagans who practised cremation in accordance with their religious belief, but these have been comparatively few. Yet, even today, in the elaborate funeral rites of many religious sects in India, China and Siam, the funeral pyre is an essential feature.

Any custom which interferes with the prescribed burial of corpses without sufficient reason, has always drawn upon itself the strict prohibition of the Church. Even the fashion of boiling the corpses or removing the bones of those who died in distant countries so as to render the body more easily portable, was strictly forbidden by Pope Boniface VIII.[5] After discussing the demerits of such a practice, which he styled abominable, he declared that any person employing such, incurred excommunication "ipso facto" reserved to the Holy See. The usage of cremation did not receive any noticeable attention from the civilized world until the 19th century. The Freemasons who assembled at Padua in 1873 instituted a campaign advocating cremation and the establishment of crematories in the larger cities. How far this project succeeded can be easily determined by examining the reports of the crematories and various cremation societies. The number of those who desired the cremation of their bodies is very scant. The statistics of Paris illustrate this remarkably. From 1889 to 1905 there were 73,000 cremations in this metropolis: only

---

3 Wernz, l. c., Tit. XVII, No. 466.

4 Acta et Decreta, Concilii Plenarii Quebecensis Prima, Tit. XIII, No. 607, sq. Catholic Encyclopedia, "Burial," "Cremation."

5 C. 1, III, 6, in Extrav. Commun.

3484 were by request: 37,082 were hospital debris: 32,757 were embryos.

Notwithstanding the apparent failure of this project, the Church continues insistent that "the bodies of the faithful departed must be buried, cremation being reprobated."[6] The reason for this strict legislation is twofold: the bodies of the faithful departed, which have been the Temples of the Holy Ghost, should be fittingly interred in consecrated ground; and since cremation is openly advocated by Masonic sects as a direct affront to the Church, it must be condemned. Furthermore, the canon states, that "should anyone in any way order his body to be cremated, this 'voluntas' is unlawful and any stipulation, will or disposition to that effect must be disregarded." Consequently, if the family or connections of the deceased propose to carry out such a wish, the Church demands that ecclesiastical burial with the funeral service be denied. The Ordinaries are directed to carefully instruct all who have any leaning to this custom or who intend to have the bodies of others cremated; the custom is to be exposed as a "detestable abuse of the human body."[7] Affiliation with societies which promote the practice of cremation is distinctly forbidden.[8] In practise however, certain contingencies may arise that demand careful attention. In this wise, a Letter of the S. Congregation of the Propagation of the Faith gave prudent counsel. In some missionary countries, the laws of caste and tribal custom have a very strong hold on the natives, even after their conversion to the Faith. Cremation is very prevalent in certain Oriental regions. Knowing, that undoubtedly the body will be cremated, the priest may hold himself passive, of course not approving at all of cremation, administer Baptism and carefully and wisely educate the people to the Christian attitude on this usage.[9]

---

6 Canon 1203, No. 1.
7 S. Cong. S. Off. 19 May, 1886=Coll. P. F. No. 1651.
8 Ibidem.
9 27 Sep. 1884=Coll. P. F. No. 1626.

SECTION I. CEMETERIES

I. Early Christian Cemeteries

For the burial of her dead, the Church has always prescribed the setting-apart and designation of places suitable for the tombs and graves. With that regard for the bodies of the faithful departed—the habitation of the rational soul, like to the image of God—and the Temple of the Holy Ghost—the law of the Church demands that the place set aside for their interment should obtain a special religious significance. The ground, venerated by the relics of martyrs and saints, was always considered as sacred and was deputed so by suitable religious rites when such were possible. These designated locations were such as the customs and times preferred. In the first years of the Christian era, the converts to the Gospel were content to have their bodies interred without distinction in the graves of their Jewish brethren.[1] It could not have been long however, before the Christians, especially those who lived where there were large Christian colonies, buried their dead in special places. The wide divergence of the Jewish and Christian idea of burial demanded distinction of location. The conflicting abhorrence and reverence held in regard to the dead body required a distinct ritual and consequently a separate burial place. In Her early days of struggle and persecution, the infant Church was not in a position to set aside and embellish cemeteries as we know them today. The earliest Christian burial places were family vaults erected on private property. From Apostolic times down to the persecution of Domitian, the faithful were interred in private burial allotments, situated like the pagan tombs along the border of the great roads and in requirement with the strict civil

1 Acts V, 6, VIII, 2 and IX, 37.

laws—outside the walls of the city.[2] These family vaults were the beginnings of those underground cemeteries which we know and revere today as the Catacombs. Contrary to an opinion which was formerly widely held—that the Christians excavated these subterranean chambers on account of the merciless persecutions levelled against them—it has been definitely established that they were commenced under no cloak of secrecy but rather enjoyed the approval and protection of the Roman government which severely prohibited any violation or interference with the cemeteries of the dead.[3] The catacomb of St. Domitilla presents a striking example of this. Situated as it was on a prominent location on the public highway of the Via Ardeatina, it possessed an entrance which could be plainly perceived from the road. "These early tombs whether above or below ground display a sense of perfect security and an absence of all fear or solicitude."[4] It was only after the Christians were driven from their more or less secret gathering places to congregate in these underground cemeteries for the performance of the rites of Religion, that the catacombs were searched and despoiled by the Roman officials in their programme of arrest and persecution. In the year 253, the Emperor Valerian published a decree whereby he sought to close against them even these subterranean retreats; he forbade them, "either to hold assemblies or to enter those places which they called their cemeteries."[5]

With the increasing numbers of their dead, the Christians enlarged their sepulchres and excavated galleries, passages, chambers, etc., in this underground area so that the catacombs assumed the vast proportions which are evident today. "The catacombs were originated from the particular tombs of the wealthy Christians who had them built in their gardens or villas.

---

2 Cath. Encyc.—"Cemeteries;" "Catacombs."
3 Moulart, "De Sepultura et Coemeteriis," pages 10-22.
4 Lanciani, "Pagan and Christian Rome," page 309.
5 Northcote, "Roman Catacombs," page 30.

In place of reserving them to their household, they permitted the use of them to their co-religionists. The inscriptions on the more ancient cemeteries in Rome confirm this opinion."[6]

Towards the end of the fourth century when the Christians were relieved of persecution, open air cemeteries were established. The vogue for these cemeteries in place of the catacombs had probably begun in Rome before the reign of Constantine.[7] Especially in Africa the findings of archeology have demonstrated this fact.[8]

In practically all of these early instances, the interment in graves was in the near neighborhood of the oratories and churches. Although Roman law had prevented burial within the walls of the city, this prohibition began to be disregarded about this time and after the pontificate of John III (560-575), it would seem that burials in Rome generally took place within the walls.[9] From this time to the present, the history of cemeteries presents but few departures from these early practises and customs.

II. Ecclesiastical Law Regarding Cemeteries

Since the burial places of the faithful are so closely connected with religion by reason of their significant character and the attendant rites and functions, the Church formulates suitable laws and regulations.

---

6 Leclercq, "Manuel d'Archéologie Chrétienne," Vol. I, pp. 323, 324.
7 Cath. Encyc. "Cemeteries."
8 Leclercq, l. c.
9 Wernz, l. c., No. 468.

CHAPTER I. RIGHTS OF THE CHURCH

1. Church and State

The authority to which the Church is entitled relative to Catholic cemeteries should not be limited by any encroachment of the State. The Catholic Church has the inherent, legitimate right fully independent from all civil power, of acquiring temporal goods necessary for Her purpose. Truly then, the cemeteries, in which the bodies of the faithful departed are laid to rest in such a becoming manner accompanied by the sacred rites, are intimately connected with the end of the Church.[1] In the first place, the character of these places is sacred. The Church demands that they be blessed according to her sacred ceremonial and to be held in reverent repute. Over "res sacrae" her dominion must be supreme. Then secondly, She has the inviolable right of preserving Her cemeteries solely for her own. A principle of canon law, as contained in the Decretals of Gregory IX states, "with those with whom we have had no communion while living, we do not communicate when dead."[2] Consequently She reserves for the faithful the title and custody of the Catholic cemeteries and permits of no trespass therein on the part of non-Catholics.[3] Notwithstanding the evident reason and justice of this claim, the civil authorities in several countries of Europe and elsewhere refuse to guarantee or even allow the Church this right, which is inherent in her very constitution.[4] Such a state of affairs is to be deplored. Pius IX in an Allocution, "Numquam Certe" delivered in a secret Consistory on the 22nd of June, 1868, brings to attention and condemns the deplorable attitude of the

1 Wernz, l. c., No. 469; Cavagnis, "Institutiones Juris Publici Ecclesiastici," Vol. III, Lib. IV, No. 278.

2 C. 12, X, III, 28.

3 Laurentius, "Institutiones Juris Canonici," No. 933.

4 Laurentius, l. c., No. 933.

Austrian Government in meddling in strictly ecclesiastical affairs so as to subject the Church in that Empire to gross indignities. The Holy Father states, "that all authority of the Church relative to Her cemeteries has been destroyed, and Catholics are compelled to admit in their cemeteries the corpses of heretics when these heretics have cemeteries of their own."[5] The Church is a perfect society and is not subject to the laws of the State. The State has no right at all to interfere with the Church's administration of "*bona ecclesiastica.*" Of course, as long as the civil statutes are in themselves just and suitable, the Church agreeably approves them.[6]

An objection may be put forth, that since sepulture is from the "jus gentium" prescribed by the law of humanity, it is to be regulated by the natural and civil order; the accompanying religious rites are only additions to it. This is not true. The Christian religion has elevated sepulture to a religious office; sepulture is considered as a "res religiosa." When the Church does not wish to extend to certain ones the religious rite of sepulture, She relinquishes them to the authority and custody of the State—then does the State care for them from the law of humanity.[7]

The State's concern regarding burial apparently arises from motives of hygiene and the public weal. To ensure sanitation and to prevent contagion and disease come within the scope of its authority and duty. Furthermore, the State has rights and obligations of guarding against any danger of premature burial and inspection of corpses in the investigation of crime. All this is quite evidently the competence of the State.[8] Nevertheless sepulture is a religious act and the cemetery is deputed a religious place. With such a significance, ecclesiastical sepulture cannot be subjected to the dictation of the State.[9] In practically all of the regions where the Church

5 Acta Sanctae Sedis, Vol. IV, p. 10.
6 Cavagnis, l. c., No. 281.
7 Cavagnis, l. c., No. 279.
8 Cavagnis, l. c., Nos. 280, 281.
9 Wernz, l. c., No. 469.

is denied her rights in burial affairs, the civil authorities and legislation are prompted principally by motives of intolerance and opposition to these prerogatives of ecclesiastical authority and competence.

The new Code reaffirms the constant contention that "the Catholic Church has the right to possess her own cemeteries," and gives the directions to be followed when this right is refused.[10]

2. Canonical Legislation

The prescriptions of this canon are fourfold to meet with the contingencies of civil requirements in various countries. 1. Whenever such is at all possible, the Church must possess and control the Catholic cemeteries so as to have full jurisdiction in regard to their sacred character, rites of blessing and burial services, to the admission of those persons who are entitled to ecclesiastical burial and to the rejection of those persons who are forbidden such or who have forfeited this right.[11] 2. When full jurisdiction is denied to the Church in regard to cemeteries which are occupied in the main by Catholics, the Ordinaries shall take care that these cemeteries shall be blessed. Formerly the law did not specifically define regulations covering this case, although it legislated definitively in regard to the reserved Catholic sections.[12] The New Code defines exactly what is to be done where the majority of persons buried are Catholics.[13] 3. Whenever it is possible, the Church should demand and obtain from the civil authorities, the reservation of a plot in the common cemeteries. This separate plot is to be reserved for Catholics and the Ordinaries are directed to have the same blessed.[14] A decree of the S. Congregation of the Propagation of the

---

10 Can. 1206.

11 Can. 1206, No. 1; S. C. S. Off., 12 Feb., 1862=Coll. P. F., No. 1227.

12 Coronata, "De Locis Sacris," No. 144.

13 Can. 1206, No. 2.

14 S. C. Prop. Fid., 29 Aug., 1763, Coll., No. 449; S. C. S. Off., 12 Feb., 1862.

Faith directed, that in the case of these cemeteries common to Catholics and non-Catholics a separate entrance is to be obtained for the reserved Catholic section.[15] 4. When all distinction or reservation of plots for Catholic burial is refused the ecclesiastical authorities, with the consequence that the blessing of the cemetery as a whole or in part is not allowed, then accordingly as each body (Catholic) is interred that single grave is to be blessed.[16] In all cases where circumstances compel the burial of Catholics in common or non-Catholic cemeteries, the Catholic rites alone must be carried out and all trace of superstition carefully avoided.[17]

CHAPTER II. BURIAL IN CHURCHES

During the first three centuries, burial in churches was practically unknown. Churches, such as they were, were few in number; the Christians were cruelly persecuted and compelled to practise great secrecy and caution in the performance of their religious rites; and the civil law absolutely forbade any interment within the city walls. However, with the triumph of Christianity the observance of this civil requirement began to be neglected, for the people desired that the remains of the holy martyrs be interred in the church building so that they might more suitably venerate these relics and flock to their tombs to beseech their heavenly intercession. Then shortly arose the custom of burying in the churches the remains of departed prelates and others who died in the odor of sanctity. Ordinarily the place of burial for interment was in the immediate vicinity of the church, but permission for burial inside them was granted for the remains of Bishops, Abbots, Priests and revered laymen. Originally, the entrance, vestibule and

15 S. C. Prop. Fid., 29 March, 1830, Coll., No. 812.
16 Can. 1206, No. 3; Rituale Romanum, Tit. VI, C. 3.
17 S. C. Prop. Fid., 29 Aug., 1763, Coll., No. 449.

porticos were the locations selected for this deposition and these places were often reserved also for Emperors and Rulers.[1] Then after a while these desired locations were allowed to the people in general, while the bodies of prelates and saintly men were admitted to burial in the churches themselves.

This custom became more widely spread and in fact, burial in the churches became less and less restricted as to the class of persons allowed such.[2] Still there is no doubt that in many places sepulture in the cemeteries was preferred.[3] In Gratian's Decretum an insert from the decrees of the Council of Nantes (658 A. D.) states that sepulture is forbidden in the church itself but permitted in the "atrium, porticos or environs of the church."[4] Likewise an insert from the Council of Mayennce declares that burial in the church is forbidden to all except Bishops, Abbots, saintly priests and noteworthy laics.[5] Nevertheless as Ferraris remarks, that in his time (early part of the 18th century) the custom had been introduced that all Catholics, clerical or lay, might be buried in the church.[6]

The Roman Ritual prescribes, that—"where the ancient custom of burying the dead in churches flourishes, the same is to be retained and where it can be done—restored."[7] This custom was more or less prevalent, according to the circumstances of place and civil law, until the end of the 18th century, when civil laws were enacted in many countries which demanded that the cemeteries be located some distance removed from the churches and outside the cities.[8] From this time on burial in churches became less and less frequent.[9]

---

1 Devoti, "Institutiones Canonicarum," Vols. II, III, Tit. IX, No. 2, Bingham, l. c., p. 58.

2 Schmalzgrueber, "Jus Ecclesiasticum Universum," Lib. III, Tom. II, Tit. XXVIII, Nos. 1, 2, 3. Reiffenstuel, l. c., Tit. XXVIII, No. 3.

3 Wernz, l. c., No. 468.

4 C. 15, C. XIII, Q. 2.

5 C. 18, C. XIII, Q. 2.

6 Ferraris, "Bibliotheca Prompta, etc.," "Sepultura," No. 5.

7 Tit. VI, C. 1, n. 9; S. C. R., 2 April, 1875, No. 3339.

8 Laurentius, l. c., No. 932.

9 Coronata, l. c., No. 136.

The New Code makes no change from the more recent legislation yet it distinctly enumerates those persons to whom burial in churches is reserved, namely: residential bishops and abbots or prelates nullius. They may be buried in their own churches. Likewise, the Roman Pontiff, Cardinals and royal personages enjoy such privilege.[10] The Ritual prescribes that when bodies of the faithful are interred in the Church, they should be placed with the feet towards the main altar, and if in oratories or chapels—with the feet towards the altar. But priests are placed with the head towards the altar.[11] The Ritual prescribes that bodies must not be interred close to the altar.[12] Various decree of the S. Congregation of Rites have determined the distance required.[13] The New Code states that no body may be interred within the distance of one meter from the altar; and thus discussion of these numerous decrees is unnecessary.[14] Note however, that if the altar is separated from the tomb by a stone chamber, although the distance be less than one meter, Mass may be said.[15] And moreover if the removal could be effected only with difficulty, the bodies may be allowed to remain undisturbed.[16] In some countries, the civil law forbids burial in churches and this statute has to be respected. This is strikingly noticeable of the city of Rome itself, where even Cardinals must be buried in the common city cemetery. The important feature to note is that the New Code forbids burial in churches to all except those especially privileged.[17] A question arose as to whether burial in an underground church is reprobated by this canon. The "Pontifical Commission for the Authentic interpretation

---

10 Can. 1205, No. 2.

11 Tit. VI, C. 1, n. 7.

12 Tit. VI, C. 1, n. 9.

13 13 Feb., 1666, n. 5, No. 1333; 7 Jul., 1766, No. 2479; 12 Jan., 1897, No. 3944; 3 Aug., 1901, No. 4082.

14 Can. 1202.

15 S. C. R., 27 Jul., 1878, ad. II, No. 3460; S. C. R., 18 Jul., 1902, No. 4100.

16 S. C. P. F., 22 Nov., 1790, ad. 3, Coll. D. F., No. 603; S. C. R., 2 Apr., 1875, No. 3339.

17 Can. 1205, No. 2.

of the Canons of the Code," decided that if this underground church is a church in the true and proper sense, used for divine worship, the law of the canon is to be applied.[18]

CHAPTER III. THE CEMETERY—A SACRED PLACE

The bodies of the faithful are to be buried in a cemetery, which must be blessed according to the rites in the approved liturgical books, either by a solemn or simple blessing, by those who have the required authorization.[1] Blessing may be defined as—"that invocation of the Divine name, by a lawful minister, made over persons or things to requests a spiritual benefit for persons or the endowment of some sacred signification."[2] A place is rendered sacred by constitutive blessing. This species of blessing is distinct by reason of the effect from invocatory blessing, i. e. which is given to houses, farms, etc.[3] Constitutive blessing may be defined as—"that invocation of the Divine Name by which persons and things are detached from profane use and their former condition, so as to be dedicated in perpetuity to Divine Cult as sacred persons and sacred things."[4] In this light we understand by the blessing of the cemetery—that segregation of the place from its former condition by rendering it a sacred place.[5] The blessing may be either solemn (consecration) or simple. The distinction is one of form.[6] In solemn blessing or consecration, a place is rendered sacred by the employment of the prayers and ceremonies with the unction of holy oil. In simple blessing, a place is rendered sacred

---

18 16 Oct., 1919=A. A. S., Vol. XI, p. 478.

---

1 Can. 1205.
2 Wernz, l. c., No. 760.
3 Noldin, "De Sacramentis," No. 52.
4 Wernz, l. c., No. 760.
5 Coronata, l. c., No. 4.
6 Wernz, l. c., No. 760; Noldin, l. c., No. 52.

by the employment of the prayers and ceremonies but without any sacred unction. Thus solemn and simple blessing have the same effect, namely that of imparting sacredness; and all blessed cemeteries enjoy the rights and privileges proper to sacred places and subject to those general prescriptions concerning sacred places.[7] Consequently one should not be surprised at the rare number of consecrated cemeteries.[8] The legislation and special instruction proper to sacred places as treated in the New Code, are to be applied also to cemeteries.[9] Hence we shall discuss only those features which have a special bearing on our subject of "Cemeteries."

1. The Minister of the Solemn Blessing or Consecration

Ordinarily, for the consecration of a sacred place the minister of this function possesses the episcopal character.

(a) Cardinals—Whether they are Bishops or not, Cardinals may validly and licitly consecrate cemeteries everywhere providing the required permission of the local Ordinary is obtained, although this requirement is for the liceity alone.[10]

(b) Bishops—The Bishop of the place may validly and licitly consecrate the cemeteries located in his diocese. A Bishop of another diocese may validly consecrate the cemetery, but for liceity he must first obtain the permission of the Ordinary of the diocese in which the cemetery is located.[11]

(c) Vicars General—Vicars General who lack the episcopal character may, by virtue of a special mandate, consecrate cemeteries. Special notice is given them in this canon.[12]

---

7 Schmalz., l. c., Tit. XL, No. 62.
8 Moulart, l. c., p. 107; Many, l. c., No. 144.
9 Cans. 1205, 1155, 1156.
10 Cans. 239, No. 1, 20'; 1157.
11 Cans. 1155, 1157.
12 Can. 1155.

(d) Vicars Capitular—The above will also apply to Vicars Capitular or Administrators, by virtue of the Canon which uses the term "Ordinary;" these dignitaries are classified as "Ordinarii loci."[13]

(e) Abbots Nullius—Lacking episcopal character, Abbots Nullius may validly and licitly consecrate cemeteries, providing they have received that blessing which the law prescribes for themselves.[14] An Apostolic prescription or a statute of their religion may require that an Abbot Nullius be blessed.[15] It must be remembered that this personal blessing is to be conferred on the Abbot by a Bishop, not by another Abbot.[16] But if an Abbot Nullius is not required by law or statute to receive this blessing, may he then consecrate cemeteries? From the tenour of the Code it appears that such would be legitimate and valid.[17]

(f) Prelates Nullius—The prescriptions of the law in this detail are identical with those concerning Abbots Nullius.[18] The same requirements and regulations are to be applied to these prelates as described in the foregoing paragraph.

(g) Priests—Simple priests may licitly and validly consecrate cemeteries only when they have received a special faculty from the Roman Pontiff. The law of consecration is of general ecclesiastical law and certainly the Roman Pontiff has the power to dispense from it, so as to allow a certain priest in a particular instance to consecrate a cemetery.[19]

(h) Permission of the Ordinary of the place. Those who are not Ordinaries may consecrate cemeteries only when the permission of the local Ordinary has been obtained.[20] Consequently, all Bishops, Cardinals, Vicars General, Abbots and the like, of a foreign diocese, must

---

13 Cans. 1156, 198, No. 1.
14 Can. 323, No. 2.
15 Can. 322, No. 2.
16 S, C. R., 8 Mar., 1617.
17 Can. 323, No. 1, No. 2.
18 Cans. 319, 323.
19 Cans. 218, 219, 1147.
20 Can. 1157.

first obtain this permission from the local Ordinary. All local Ordinaries may grant this permission whether or not they themselves have episcopal character.[21] The Ordinary of the place may be—the Roman Pontiff, diocesan Bishop, Vicar General, Abbot or Prelate Nullius, Administrator, Vicar or Prefect Apostolic.[22] Also those personages other than the prelates listed, who in the meanwhile have succeeded in the position of authority by reason of prescription of law or approved custom. Likewise the Major Superior of exempt clerical communities, are the Ordinaries for their subjects in religion. The Ordinaries granting permission and those receiving it must be of the same rite.[23] Consequently, a Latin Ordinary may not grant permission to a Ruthenian Bishop to consecrate a cemetery. If such took place, the consecration would be valid but illicit. Major Superiors are the Ordinaries for their religious subjects. Now, are they allowed to call in and grant permission to a foreign prelate to consecrate their cemeteries? The canon in treating of the required permission mentions only, "Ordinarii," not "Ordinarii loci."[24] Yet the Code has stated that the consecration of a sacred place pertains to the Ordinary of that place.[25] With this in mind the more suitable procedure to follow would be for the Religious to first ask the Ordinary of that place to consecrate their cemetery. However, if he should not comply with their request, then after six months delay, the Major Superior would have every right to call in a strange Ordinary.[26] Of course this is applicable only in the case of exempt Religious.

---

21 Can. 1155, No. 2.
22 Can. 198, No. 1.
23 Can. 1155, No. 2.
24 Can. 1157.
25 Can. 1155, No. 1.
26 Many, l. c., No. 12; Coronata, l. c., No. 5.

(1) *Minister of the Simple Blessing*

For validity, priestly character alone is required. For liceity, there are definite regulations for special cases.[27]

(a) The Ordinary of the place—The simple blessing pertains to the Ordinary of the place for all the cemeteries in his diocese, excepting those which belong to exempt Religious.[28]

(b) Major Superior—The simple blessing of a cemetery belonging to exempt Religious, pertains to the Major Superior.[29]

(c) Priest—Any priest may be delegated by the Ordinary of the place to bless the cemetery.[30] Likewise the Major Superior may delegate any priest to bless the cemetery belonging to the exempt Religious.[31] Either permission is required for the liceity, notwithstanding any privilege to the contrary.[32]

2. Registration of the Blessing

When a cemetery has been solemnly or simply blessed, a document must be drawn up concerning the function—one copy of which, is to be reserved in the parochial archives; and another sent to the Diocesan Chancery.[33] In regards to the cemeteries of exempt Religious, one copy will be kept in the Church of the Religious—but what of the other copy? Coronata states that it would not be required to send it to the Diocesan Chancery, but simply send it to the Provincial or General House of the Order. The Code makes no provision for this case, and simply makes the statement, that "a copy must be kept in the diocesan curia." Prudence and

27 Can. 1147, No. 3; Wernz, l. c., Tom. II, No. 158.
28 Cans. 1156, 1205.
29 Can. 1156.
30 Can. 1156.
31 Can. 1156.
32 Can. 1157.
33 Can. 1158.

courtesy should suggest the preferable mode of procedure.

3. Proof of the Blessing

The documents are certain proofs of the blessing. If such could not be discovered, then various evidences or attestations would be sufficient to indicate that the cemetery once had been blessed, such as—crosses and chapels situated in the cemetery. The testimony of one witness (unprejudiced) could sufficiently establish such proof.[34] The blessing, whether solemn or simple, must not be repeated. However if no legal proof or deposition could be obtained, the cemetery may then be blessed.[35] If there is doubt, it may be blessed, "ad cautelam."[36] It is not so much that the doubt of the blessing would necessitate the function, but rather that the contrary be proven.[37]

4. Special Exceptions to the Law

The Church is very insistent that the bodies of the departed faithful be interred in sacred ground, yet for certain reasons, She allows of departures from this law. Thus, in more or less uncivilized countries where customs and formalisms retain such a hold on the natives, the burial of the bodies of Christians in pagan tombs and graves was tolerated to avoid scandal and greater evil.[38]

In civilized countries certain contingencies may arise which demand exception from the law of the Church. In a certain case, the Ordinary may permit of the burial of a Catholic in a civil or even in a sectarian cemetery. The III Council of Baltimore recognized the advisability of such procedure in the case of a recent

34 Can. 1159, No. 1; C. 16, D. 1, de Consec.; S. R. C., 19 Aug., 1634, No. 611.

35 Can. 1159, No. 2.

36 Can. 1159, No. 2.

37 Gasparri, "De SSma. Euchåristia," No. 151; Coronata, l. c., No. 8.

38 Constitution of Bened. XIV, "Inter Omnigenas," 2 Feb., 1744=Coll. P. F., No. 345; S. C. S. Off., 13 April, 1853=Coll. P. F., No. 1089; S. C. P. F., 20 Feb., 1801=Coll. P. F., No. 649 and No. 650.

convert to the Faith, whose non-Catholic relatives would demand interment in their family vault located in civil or sectarian cemetery.[39] The Catholic in question has not been guilty of this disobedience of the law of the Church—probably he had even preferred burial in the Catholic cemetery. For this reason he should not be denied the funeral rites and burial service, if such can be celebrated without serious interference on the part of the non-Catholic family. The pastor must consult the Ordinary in all such eventualities, who will prudently advise him just what should be done.

In regards to the deposition of dismembered parts of the body following surgical operations, the Sisters in charge of hospitals were in doubt. They asked of the S. Congregation of the Holy Office just what they should do and what they should allow others do with these organs and members. The S. Congregation replied that if possible these dismembered portions (of Catholic patients) should be buried in the cemeteries; but if this would be difficult and inconvenient, the Sisters may continue their practice of simply interring them in a profane place. When the surgeons directed them to have them burned, the Sisters should, for the sake of prudence, follow out their orders. The S. Congregation gave this counsel—that if such were possible, a place annexed to the institution should be set aside for this purpose of burying the amputated members and organs, and this place should be blessed.[40]

As we have already mentioned (page 8), in some countries Catholics are not allowed to possess a cemetery for their special use. In such places, where the cemeteries as a whole or in part, cannot be blessed the ecclesiastical law prescribes that the graves are to be singly blessed accordingly as each Catholic burial occurs.[41]

---

39 Acta et Decreta, III Plen. Council Baltimore, Tit. XI, No. 317.

40 S. C. S. Off., 3 April, 1897=Coll. P. F., No. 1975.

41 Can. 1206, No. 3; Wernz, l. c., Nos. 468, 470; Devoti, l. c., Tit. IX, No. II; D'Angelo, "Della Sepoltura Ecclesiastica," Cap. 5.

CHAPTER IV. INTERDICT OF THE CEMETERY

Cemeteries may be placed under an interdict by competent authority.[1] This local interdict may be either—general, i. e., inflicted on a whole province, diocese, city or village—or particular, i. e., inflicted on individual sacred places.[2] Before the New Code, when a place was placed under a general local interdict, ecclesiastical burial was forbidden indiscriminately to all laics in this territory. The clerics, who were entirely inculpable of this penalty, had a privilege of burying their dead in the cemeteries, but without any solemnization of rites.[3] The New Code has changed this and allows burial in the cemeteries of places interdicted by a general penalty, to all clerics and laics, unless they themselves have been personally interdicted also.[4] This burial must not be accompanied by external solemnity. Likewise, before the New Code, if the interdict was a particular one, ecclesiastical burial was forbidden to all laics with a like exception for the clerics. But the New Code changes this distinctly by stating that, "if a cemetery was interdicted, the bodies of the faithful may be interred therein, but without any ecclesiastical rite."[5]

CHAPTER V. VIOLATION OF THE CEMETERY

By violation, or pollution—as it was called in the old law—the cemetery is so defiled that it is rendered unfit for ecclesiastical burial with the attendant rites and functions. Violation is a moral contamination of the sacredness of the cemetery by certain acts of an indecent

1 Can. 2269.
2 Sole, "De Delictis et Poenis," Tit. VIII, No. 234.
3 Wernz, l. c., Vol. VI, No. 228.
4 Cans. 2270, 2271.
5 Can. 2272, No. 2.

or illicit nature.[1] The four species of sordid offense which cause the violation of the church, likewise cause the violation of the cemetery.[2] In the old law it was the unanimous opinion that cemeteries were polluted in the same way as churches.[3] However then, the legislation required that the violation of the church "ipso facto" caused the violation of the cemetery contiguous, and vice versa that of the cemetery caused the pollution of the church. The new Code changes this by explicitly stating that the violation of the cemetery does not follow from the violation of the church.[4] The four species of sordid offense which cause the violation of the cemetery, are as follows—criminal homicide, injurious and serious shedding of blood, impious and sordid practices to which the cemetery had been converted, and the burial of an infidel or a person who had been excommunicated after a declaratory or condemnatory sentence.

1. Necessary Conditions

The Code specifies certain defined conditions under which these offenses must have taken place to constitute violation.[5] If these conditions or circumstances are not verified, then no violation can be imputed to the cemetery. Consequently we have a clear rule to follow and former uncertainty and misunderstanding have been removed.

(1) *The offense must have been certain*

The offense committed must be certain both "de jure," i. e. that the act committed constitutes by law a violation, and certain "de facto," i. e. that such an offense had really been committed. This condition has always been insisted upon by ecclesiastical law. Thus

1 Bargilliat, "Praelectiones Juris Canonici," Cap. 2, Art. 5.

2 Can. 1207, 1172.

3 C. 7, XIII, 40; C. 1, III, 21, in Vito; Reiffenstuel, l. c., Tom. IV, Tit. XL, No. 15; Schmalzgrueber, l. c., Tit. XL, No. 63 and No. 72; Ferraris, l. c., "Ecclesia," No. 30; Moulart, l. c., p. 118, sq.; Wernz, l. c., Tom. III, No. 445 and No. 471.

4 Can. 1172, No. 2.

5 Can. 1172, No. 1.

is it apparent that if there is any doubt, either of law or of fact, the integrity of the cemetery must be presumed until the contrary has been satisfactorily established.[6]

(2) *The offense must have been notorious*

It may be notorious either of fact or of law.[7] The stain which the cemetery suffers from violation is not so much the desecration itself, but principally the fact of this being known notoriously and thus regarded as an opprobrium, an outrage to the sacred dignity and reverence due to this sacred place. Then, as long as an offense would remain occult or even public—in the canonical sense, and not made notorious by those persons who witnessed it, the reconciliation of the cemetery would not be required.[8] The fact may be known only to one person or even to two or three who are not likely to broadcast it. Then it is considered occult and would not constitute the violation. The fact may be public, i. e.—known to several persons but not notorious nor considered so by those who know of it.[9] Consequently, there must be notoriety of fact, or notoriety of law, i. e.—after a juridical sentence has so declared it or after a confession made in court in the presence of a judge with all the formalities required to give it judicial character.[10]

(3) *The offense must have been performed in the cemetery itself*

Little discussion is necessary regarding this detail. It is evident that the cemetery comprises a certain defined area, in practically every instance, enclosed by a wall or fence. If the offense occurred one inch outside the cemetery area violation of the cemetery would not follow. A civil public cemetery in which the graves are

6 Gasparri, l. c., No. 246.
7 Can. 2197.
8 Coronata, l. c., No. 197.
9 Sole, l. c., No. 9 and No. 10; Ayrinhac, "Penal Legislation," p. 28, No. 6.
10 Can. 2197; 1750; Sole, l. c., No. 6; Ayrinhac, l. c., p. 29, n. c.

blessed singly cannot be violated in this canonical sense since it has not been blessed as a cemetery. According to a probable opinion, violation cannot be imputed to those civil cemeteries in which are buried a majority of Catholics, although these cemeteries have been blessed as required by the New Code.[11]

2. Offenses Causing Violation

(1) *The crime of homicide*

This has always constituted violation and was taken in its strict sense—the killing of a human being.[12] The New Code makes it clear that to induce violation, the homicide must have been criminal—advertently and wilfully perpetrated. Accidental killing or such perpetrated by an infant or insane person would not constitute violation. If committed by one under the influence of liquor, it would depend upon whether he in any way foresaw the act or not to constitute the crime of homicide.[13] The killing of an aggressor in self-defense involves no crime and consequently no violation if it occurred in the cemetery. If one received a mortal wound outside and then enters the cemetery and dies, there would be no violation, for the law distinctly requires this act to have happened within the cemetery confines—death alone is not sufficient. Likewise, if one had received a mortal wound in the cemetery and then departed and died outside, the cemetery would not have been violated (unless on account of the other cause, i. e., shedding of blood, as we will discuss in the next paragraph). Formerly this was not so clearly established but the New Code leaves no room for doubt.[14] Homicide perpetrated by one stationed outside the cemetery on one inside it, would cause its violation. Suicide, and even

11 Can. 1206, No. 2; Wernz, l. c., No. 471; Coronata, l. c., No. 146, 2'.
12 C. 19 and 20; D. 1, de Consec.
13 Gasp., l. c., No. 259.
14 Moulart, l. c., p. 121; Can. 1172.

martyrdom, would produce the same result of violation if such occurred in the cemetery.

(2) *Injurious and grave shedding of blood*

The "effusio sanguinis" mentioned in the old law has always been interpreted as referring to a copious flow of human blood caused by a voluntary, injurious and gravely sinful action.[15] The new Code affirms and mentions these special conditions explicitly.[16] An abundant flow of blood is required to cause violation; a few drops, or the oozing of blood from a light wound would not. It is left to the prudent judgment of mankind to determine this. Authors disputed as to whether a copious nose-bleed resultant from a blow inflicted in a quarrel would be termed an injurious and gravely sinful shedding of blood.[17] They are agreed that such resulting from a scuffle between two children is not gravely sinful and therefore not a violation. Such occurring in a fight between two adults of over fourteen years of age, might cause violation. But in such an instance it must be taken into consideration whether the injured party was really hurt and whether the witnesses of this act look upon it as a serious irreverence and outrage done to the cemetery. The blood, of course, must be that of a human being and the act injurious and gravely sinful—as we have discussed in "homicide."

(3) *Impious and sordid usages to which the cemetery had been subjected*

The New Code here makes a departure from the former legislation. The old law enumerated as one of the acts which cause violation, the "effusio seminis."[18] The glossators and later commentators interpreted this as adultery, fornication, pollution, sodomy and such

---

15 C. 20, D. 1, de Consec.; Ferraris, l. c., "Ecclesia," No. 26; Gasparri, l. c., No. 251.

16 Can. 1172, No. 1, 2°.

17 Schmalzgrueber, l. c., Tit. XL, No. 79; Reiffenstuel, l. c., Tit. XL, No. 19; Ferraris, l. c., "Ecclesia," No. 26; Moulart, l. c., p. 122.

18 C. 20, D. I, de Consec.; C. 5, X, V, 16; C. 1, III, 21, in Vito.

abominations, voluntarily committed. Even lawful intercourse of married persons was at one time considered as inducing violation.[19] However the New Code in enumerating the causes makes no mention of such acts (considered individually) as inducing the violation. A new phrase is inserted—"impious and sordid uses."[20] In an article in the "Irish Ecclesiastical Record" this detail is treated with excellent precision and interpretation. "Instead of the 'effusio seminis humani' of the old law, we now read, 'unholy or sordid uses to which the church has been subjected,' partially more strict, since it extends the classes of acts that may lead to the result: partially more liberal, since it implies that the acts must have been performed repeatedly."[21] Thus it appears quite probable that an indecent act, such as fornication, even though it is gravely sinful and abhorrent, no longer constitutes the violation of the cemetery. Such acts happening as separate individual instances could hardly be intended by the term, "sordid uses."

(4) *Burial of an infidel or excommunicated person, after a declaratory or condemnatory sentence*

a. Infidels

In the Decretum of Gratian it is stated that a church in which a pagan has been buried does not permit of consecration nor may Mass be celebrated therein, but it is necessary that the body be removed and the church cleansed of the desecration. And again, "it is unlawful to sanctify a church in which have been buried the bodies of infidels."[22] Concerning these texts of the Decretum, there is reason to doubt their authenticity; and more so, the attributing of them to Councils of the Church. It has been established that the first one should be attributed to one "Theodorus Cantuariensis" and the latter

---

19 Ferraris, l. c., "Ecclesia," No. 49; Moulart, l. c., p. 123; Gasparri, l. c., 5.

20 Can. 1172, No. 1, 3'.

21 Irish Ecclesiastical Record, June, 1919.

22 C. 27, D. I, de Consec.; C. 28, D. I, de Consec.

to the "Capitularibus Regum Francorum."[23] For this reason, commentators in the past have strongly disputed as to whether the burial of infidels caused the violation of the church.[24] Some argued against, saying that, although such burial was illicit yet it did not pollute the church so that all that was required was the removal of the corpse.[25] It was admitted by all, that under the name of infidels, catechumens were not included. But it was disputed regarding the burial of infants of baptized parents who had died without Baptism.[26] However the New Code decides the matter definitely by stating simply that the burial of infidels in the cemetery causes its violation.[27] And by infidels are meant all who have not received the Sacrament of Baptism. But the burial of catechumens (who have not been baptized) would not cause the violation of the cemetery. The New Code states explicitly that they are allowed ecclesiastical sepulture.[28] This question was disputed in the past, although the the general and more probable opinion anticipated the present legislation.[29] Likewise the burial of unbaptised infants of Catholic parents would not cause the violation of the cemetery.[30]

b. "Excommunicati"

Prior to the New Code, there were diverse opinions as to the classes of excommunicated persons, whose burial caused the violation of the church, and likewise the violation of the cemetery. The most common opinion was that only "excommunicati vitandi" were meant.[31] In the time of Innocent III, the burial of excommunicated

---

23 Gasparri, l. c., No. 253.
24 Ojetti, l. c., No. 1927.
25 Gasparri, l. c., No. 253; Moulart, l. c., p. 124, sq.
26 Ferraris, l. c., No. 52; Gasparri, l. c., No. 253.
27 Can. 1172, No. 1, 4'.
28 Can. 1239, No. 2.
29 Schmalz., l. c., Tit. XL, No. 72; Reiff., l. c., Tit. XL, No. 77; Moulart, l. c., p. 125; Many, l. c., No. 217; Wernz, l. c., No. 442; Gasparri, l. c., No. 253.
30 Gasparri, l. c., No. 254; Wernz, l. c., No. 781, Not. 47; Coronata, l. c., No. 256.
31 Ferraris, l. c., No. 54.

persons, without any exception, caused the violation of the cemetery. But since then has been made the distinction between "vitandi" and "tolerati." Then arose the discussion as to whether "tolerati" were included in the law of violation. The more common opinion was that their burial would not cause it.[32] Yet against this, a decree of the S. Cong. of Rites in 1875 declared that the church was violated by the burial of non-Catholics, and they are "tolerati."[33] However the New Code settles the matter and states succinctly that violation caused solely by those persons who have been excommunicated by a declaratory or condemnatory sentence.[34] The distinction in the New Code is made between "tolerati simpliciter" and "tolerati post sententiam declaratoriam vel condemnatoriam."[35] Consequently, the burial of baptized non-Catholics would not cause the violation of the cemetery, unless they had been previously excommunicated by a declaratory or condemnatory sentence.

3. Consequences of Violation

(1) *Burial forbidden*

If a cemetery has been violated, burial therein is forbidden to the faithful until it has been reconciled by the prescribed ritual of the Church.[36]

(2) *Exhumation of bodies*

When a cemetery has been violated by the burial of an infidel or excommunicated person, the body or bodies must be exhumed and transferred from the cemetery before it may be reconciled. The New Code prudently adds—"if such removal can be effected without great inconvenience."[37]

---

32 Ferraris, l. c., No. 54.
33 April 23, 1875, No. 3344; Gasparri, l. c., No. 254.
34 Can. 2258.
35 Can. 2259, No. 2.
36 Rit. Rom. Tit. VIII, C. 30.
37 Can. 1175.

(3) *Penalties for violators*

The church punishes persons who have violated a cemetery, by placing such a one under an interdict forbidding him to enter the church, besides the other penalties which may be inflicted on him by the Ordinary, according to the gravity of the delinquency.[38]

(4) *Effect of the violation*

By violation the cemetery does not lose its sacred character. Consecration or benediction is lost only by execration. Execration follows when the Ordinary of the place converts the cemetery to profane uses.[39] It would also follow, if the remains have been transferred to another location; also if untoward circumstances, such as an earthquake, would render it entirely unsuitable for interment purposes; or if the civil authorities would counsel or permit the erection of buildings or the construction of roads on the property.[40]

4. Practical Conclusions

It is worthy of note that the principle, "odiosa restringenda sunt," must be applied to each and every case of violation.[41] Violation of the cemetery may be imputed only when the acts specified in the law, have really occurred and when they have taken place with the fulfillment of the conditions demanded by law, which have been treated above in this article. Even though acts have taken place in the cemetery, which seem just as desecrating or even more so, than the acts specified, nevertheless the principle, that violation must not be extended from case to case, must always be carried out. No analogy may be admitted. With this in mind, the instances of real, canonical violation will hardly be frequent. True, the law is strict and apparent, yet the necessary conditions and limitations are such that will allow of its application in rare contingencies.

---

38 Can. 2329.
39 Cans. 1170, 1187.
40 Coronata, l. c., No. 147.
41 Regula Juris, No. 15, in Vito.

CHAPTER VI. RECONCILIATION OF THE CEMETERY

The New Code contains no special regulations concerning the reconciliation of cemeteries but states that the prescriptions concerning the reconciliation of churches are also to be applied to cemeteries.[1] By reconciliation a violated cemetery is restored to its former undefiled condition, cleansed of its pollution, and rendered fit for the purpose and rites of ecclesiastical burial. Reconciliation is necessary only when the violation is certain.[2] Reconciliation is not a re-consecration or re-blessing; the cemetery does not suffer the loss of its sacredness by being violated. However, in case of doubt, the New Code prescribes that reconciliation may be performed, "ad cautelam.[3] To prevent delay and interruption of the ecclesiastical rites, reconciliation should be performed as soon as possible.[4]

1. Solemn Reconciliation

If the cemetery had been solemnly blessed (consecrated) the rite for its reconciliation is that prescribed and described in the Roman Pontifical.[5] The minister of the ceremony, may be either the Ordinary of the place, or the Major Superior for the exempt cemeteries of his Order. Either of these ministers may delegate any priest to perform the ceremony.[6] Under the old law, the reconciliation of consecrated churches and likewise that of consecrated cemeteries was reserved to the Ordinary.[7] This was expressly stated in the Decretal of

1 Cans. 1207, 1174, 1177.
2 Wernz, l. c., No. 444.
3 Can. 1174, No. 2.
4 Can. 1174, No. 1.
5 Tit. "de ecclesiae et coemeterii reconciliatione;" Tit. "de reconciliatione coemetrii sine ecclesiae reconciliatione."
6 Cans. 1156, 1176, No. 2.
7 Ferraris, l. c., "Ecclesia," No. 66; Ojetti, l. c., No. 1930.

Gregory IX, "simple priests are prohibited from doing this, notwithstanding any custom to the contrary."[8] Only the Roman Pontiff could delegate a priest for this function and this was but rarely granted.[9] However, the New Code has extended the valid reconciliation of consecrated cemeteries to all who may be the ministers of the blessing.[10] Consequently the Ordinary of the place or the Major Superior in the case of exempt cemeteries, may delegate any priest for the function.[11] Moreover, the New Code decrees, that in case of grave or urgent necessity, if the Ordinary cannot be reached, the rector of a consecrated church may reconcile it and inform the Ordinary of it afterwards.[12] The same rule applies for cemeteries. Whether or not he be informed, of course, does not affect the validity of this reconciliation.

2. Simple Reconciliation

If the cemetery had been simply blessed, then the rite of reconciliation is that contained in the Roman Ritual.[13] Formerly it was disputed as to whether the priest required the permission of the Bishop to perform this reconciliation.[14] Yet the Ritual explicitly demands that the priest be delegated by the Ordinary.[15] No definite decision had been arrived at in this matter and it was concluded that, in practise, it was the safe and sure procedure for the priest to seek and obtain this delegation from the Bishop.[16] But now it has been decided that a blessed cemetery may be reconciled by the rector of the parish or the chaplain of the cemetery, or by any priest with at least the presumed consent of

---

8 C. 10, XIII, 41.
9 Gasparri, l. c., No. 256; Ojetti, l. c., No. 1930.
10 Can. 1176, No. 2.
11 Can. 1156.
12 Can. 1176, No. 3.
13 Tit. VIII, C. 30.
14 Devoti, l. c., Tit. IX, No. XX; Ferraris, l. c., "Ecclesia," No. 71; Many, l. c., No. 42; Ojetti, l. c., No. 1930.
15 Tit. VIII, C. 30.
16 Gasparri, l. c., No. 257.

one of these. This makes it simple and allows of wide liberty. No dignity or delegation is required, and the consent of the rector or chaplain, may be lawfully presumed unless it has been positively forbidden by him, or unless one is convinced that he (the rector or chaplain) intends to perform the rite himself.[17]

3. Church and Cemetery Adjoining

In the case, which nowadays is rare, that the cemetery adjoins the church, there arises several particular contingencies.

(1) *Both solemnly blessed*

If both church and cemetery were violated, and both had been solemnly blessed—then the rite of reconciliation is that contained in the Pontifical, and the minister of solemn reconciliation as described above.

(2) *But one solemnly blessed*

If both church and cemetery had been violated and but one solemnly blessed, then the same procedure should be observed as in No. (1), unless a double formula is used by the minister.[18]

(3) *Both simply blessed*

If both church and cemetery were violated and both had been simply blessed, then the rite to be used is that of the Ritual.[19]

N. B.=It must be remembered that the violation of one does not follow from the violation of the other.[20]

---

17 Can. 1176, No. 1; Coronata, l. c., No. 148.
18 Coronata, l. c., No. 148.
19 Tit. VII, C. 28.
20 Can. 1176, No. 2.

CHAPTER VII. IMMUNITY OF THE CEMETERY

From the old law, it is clear that churches and cemeteries enjoyed like immunity.[1] When the Church was allowed all her rights and due privileges, the cemeteries were revered as sacred places, and the civil authorities cooperated with the Church in preserving these holy places from any indignity or trespass. In recent years the State, by introducing civil, public cemeteries, and by hampering considerably the jurisdiction of the Church, has encroached upon the authority and rights of the Church so as to allow very little immunity to the cemeteries. For this reason, the New Code makes no explicit reference to immunity of cemeteries.[2] Nevertheless, from the Divine Law, special prerogatives of the cemeteries are more or less recognizd by the State.

1. Dignity of this Sacred Place

Cemeteries are protected from profane acts, and especially from any dishonest or degrading circumstances. The degree of this protection varies with amount of respect which the State gives to the Church and her constitution. Whenever the Church enjoys unrestricted control over her cemeteries, the dignity is assured; wherever she is hampered, the cemeteries are held in lesser repute by the State, and consequently indignities occur over which the Church has no authority or control.[3]

2. "Jus Asyli"

In the law of the Decretals, the same privilege of "jus asyli," or right of refuge, was attached to ceme-

---

1 C. 13, XIII, 28.
2 Coronata, l. c., No. 149.
3 Wernz, l. c., No. 472; Coronata, l. c., No. 149.

teries as to that of churches.[4] This privilege or quality was considered applicable to all blessed cemeteries, whether they were contiguous to the church or not.[5] In the Constitution of Pius IX, "Apostolicae Sedis," an excommunication "latae sententiae" simply reserved to the Roman Pontiff, was incurred by the violators of ecclesiastical asylum.[6] In a letter of the congregation of the Holy Office, notice was given that this censure was applicable to those who ordered or contrived such violation.[7] However, as Wernz remarks, "in our time, many cemeteries certainly do not enjoy this prerogative (jus asyli) since so many are merely civil cemeteries, or at least have not been established or blessed by the authority of the Bishop."[8] The New Code makes no mention of this right in regards to cemeteries—while that pertaining to churches is distinctly stressed.[9] No penalty is listed for the violators of the "jus asyli" of churches or cemeteries. Yet, it would only appear compatible that a vestige of this "jus asyli" of cemeteries remain, insofar that care should be employed—in regards to those Catholic cemeteries which enjoy their due rights and privileges—in the matter of apprehending and deporting criminals who have fled to the cemetery, so that there would be avoided and prevented any unseemly profanation of this holy ground.[10]

3. Reverence for the Remains

The prime object in the establishment of her cemeteries is the reverence which the Church desires to be shown the earthly remains of the faithful departed. With the bestowal of the last rites, the body is laid to rest in the cemetery where it receives the generous care of Her supervision. The corpses should

4 C. 5, 10, XIII, 49.
5 Schmalzgrueber, l. c., Tit. XLIX, No. 107.
6 12 Oct., 1869=Coll. P. F., No. 1348.
7 10 Feb., 1871=Coll. P. F., No. 1366.
8 Wernz, l. c., No. 472.
9 Can. 1179.
10 Coronata, l. c., No. 149.

not be exhumed except with great care and serious reason. The cemetery would be gravely desecrated if the bodies of the faithful departed should be carelessly, impiously or dishonestly exhumed or transferred.[11] The New Code demands that the permission of the Bishop be obtained before exhumation take place.[12]

N. B.=It must be noted that this prerogative of immunity belongs only to the Catholic cemeteries, or, at least, to those cemeteries which have been blessed according to the rites of the Church. From this blessing, a cemetery receives its sacred character and the consequent effects—one of which, is this ecclesiastical immunity.

CHAPTER VIII. POSSESSION OF THE CEMETERY

1. Cemeteries Properly So-Called

Cemeteries which are blessed fall under the dominion of the Church. In places where the State does not obstruct this right of the Church, certain regulations are to be observed.

(1) *Parish Cemeteries*

Each parish should have its own cemetery, unless the Ordinary of the place assigns a common cemetery to several parishes.[1] In different countries, differences in the location and style of the burial places may be noted. Except in the cities the cemetery very often adjoins the church. Thus each parish church had its own burying ground, in the recent past. In country places this may be remarked today. For various reasons the custom has arisen that the cemeteries be

---

11 Wernz, l. c., No. 472.
12 Can. 1214.

---

1 Can. 1208, No. 1.

located in the outskirts or secluded open spaces of the cities and towns. Civil requirements of sanitation have demanded this regulation; and of course, there is nothing undesirable in such a by-law from the ecclesiastical standpoint, as long as the Church is left free to control Her cemeteries exclusively. For this reason then it is often more suitable and convenient for a common cemetery to supply the needs of several parishes, which is the general rule in America. Of course, a sufficient number of cemeteries should be located so as to prevent useless inconvenience, especially in the case of poor people.[2]

The Third Council of Baltimore prescribed that, "in order to entirely prevent any danger of unjust alienation, no priest, unless he has the written permission of the Ordinary, may retain to himself (hold in his own name) either the church . . . . or cemetery . . . . for which the faithful have contributed money, but he should, as soon as possible, transfer the title to the Ordinary or to a sanctioned corporation." If the priest should retain this title in his own name for three months, the Council directs the Bishop to impose canonical penalties as listed in the various diocesan statutes.[3]

(2) *Private Cemeteries of Exempt Religious*

Exempt Religious are permitted by Church law to have their own cemeteries for their private use.[4] This privilege is of long standing. Gregory IX wrote in severe reproof of those avaricious, overbearing prelates who, among other things, compelled the Religious to bury their departed brethren in their (the prelates') churches—which was acting directly contrary to their rule which had received official approbation from the Holy See.[5] Likewise in the collection of

---

2 Acta et Decreta, II, Plen. Conc. Balt., No. 395.
3 Acta et Decreta, No. 280.
4 Can. 1208, No. 2.
5 C. 16, XV, 31.

Clement V and the "Extravagantes Communes," are found condemnations of those unauthorized prelates interfering with the burial places of Religious.[6] The New Code extends to exempt Religious not only the permission, but the right to possess their own cemeteries.[7] Moreover, these cemeteries are exempt from the visitation of the Ordinary of the place, if they were reserved to the Religious only.[8] Non-exempt Religious have no right to special cemeteries, but they can obtain permission from the local Ordinary to have private burial plots or sections reserved to them in the local cemetery.[9]

2. Private Burial Places

(1) *To Whom Conceded*

The Ordinary may allow of special or private burial places situated apart in the common cemetery, which are blessed like the cemetery. This permission may be granted to—"personae morales." By this indication, the Ordinary could permit non-exempt communities of Religious of men or women, to have their own burial sections reserved to them. Confraternities, tertiary societies, and all such groups to which the term "personae morales" may be applied, can be permitted to enjoy this privilege.[10] Even families may be permitted by the Ordinary to set apart special burying places for their private use.[11]

(2) *Conditions of Ownership*

Private lots or vaults may be allowed the faithful on certain conditions.

---

6 C. 2, III, 7, in Clem.; C. 1, II, 1, in Extrav. Commun.

7 Can. 1208, No. 2.

8 Constitution of Leo XIII, "Romani Pontifices," 8 May, 1881= Coll. D. F., No. 1552.

9 Can. 1208, No. 3.

10 Ibidem.

11 Ibidem.

a. In parochial cemeteries—The faithful are permitted to construct these special burying locations in the parochial cemeteries. And in this case the written consent of the local Ordinary must be obtained.[12]

b. In private cemeteries—If they are to be constructed in those special burial places which are reserved to exempt Religious, then the written consent of the Superior of the Order must be obtained.[13]

c. In blessed civil cemeteries—Likewise in regard to those civil cemeteries which have been blessed, the aforegoing conditions must be observed. The State in usurping the right of the Church might forbid this grant.

d. Alienation—These private locations may be alienated providing the consent of the Ordinary has been obtained, or the consent of the Major Superior—in the case of the exempt Religious cemeteries.[14] Consequently they who have obtained this privilege are permitted to transfer the ownership of their private burial places to others. There is nothing to prevent these owners from selling their plots to others. The consent of the Ordinary or of the Major Superior must be obtained for all cases of alienation.[15] There need be no apprehension that there would be a suspicion of simony resulting from a transaction of this sort. The persons who have obtained this privilege of private sepulture, have a dominative right over these special locations, lots or vaults.[16] By alienation they hand over or sell this right to others, not in any way by reason of the blessing attached, but because of the fact that the exclusive right to a determined and honorable place has a material value.[17]

---

12 Can. 1209, No. 1.
13 Ibidem.
14 Can. 1209, No. 1.
15 Ibidem.
16 Coronata, l. c., No. 142.
17 Augustine, "Commentary on Canon Law," page 111.

3. Reservation of Special Plots

(1) *For Clerics*

Special burial places should be set aside for the priests and clerics. They should be located in a more prominent part of the cemetery and separated from the plots of the lay people. And, if such can be conveniently arranged, one section should be for the priests and another for the lesser clerics.[18] The New Code repeats the text of the Roman Ritual almost verbatim.[19] The wording of the canon does not induce a strict obligation to procure this arrangement, but simply prescribes it as more befitting as long as such can be effected conveniently.[20]

(2) *For Baptised Infants*

Special locations should be set apart for the burial of the remains of infants.[21] Again the New Code repeats the text of the Ritual.[22] For the sake of the traditional and laudable practice, this procedure should be followed out if it can be conveniently arranged as there is a special set of ceremonies and prayers in the Ritual for the burial of infants.[23] Only those infants who had been baptised are entitled to burial in these special places. There is yet another arrangement to be followed for unbaptised infants. By the term, infants, not only are babies meant, but in the canonical sense, also those children who died before arriving at the age of reason.[24] A decree of the S. Congregation of Rites prescribed that exempt Religious who have allowed others to be buried in their private cemeteries, should also set apart lots for the burial of children.[25]

---

18 Can. 1209, No. 2.
19 Tit. VI, C. 1, No. 10.
20 Coronata, l. c., No. 140 (a).
21 Can. 1209, No. 3.
22 Tit. VI, C. 6, No. 1.
23 Tit. VI, C. 7.
24 Can. 88, No. 3.
25 12 Dec., 1620, No. 383.

(3) *For "Indigni."*

Ecclesiastical burial is not conceded to all simply because they are Catholics. Certain unworthy persons are denied this privilege. "If while living, they were not in communion with us, neither then should they associate with us when dead."[26] Nevertheless, the Church is a benign and loving Mother and does not refuse the offices of piety and humanity even to her undeserving children. And yet, a distinction must be provided. Consequently, the law states, that besides the blessed cemetery, another place should be designated, enclosed and protected as the cemetery, where they may be buried who are denied ecclesiastical sepulture.[27] Those denied are of two classes—the unbaptised, and certain delinquents. For unbaptised infants a special place should be set aside and another for those delinquents.[28] Of course it is to be noted that these segregated places are located apart from the cemetery and are not blessed.[29] The Council of Quebec prescribed, that, "following the tradition of the Church, a special place for the interment of the corpses of unbaptised children should be located apart, although within the cemetery confines."[30] If such an arrangement cannot be had, then these persons may be buried in the cemetery with the omission of the funeral rites. Such is intended by the words, "si haberi queat."[31] In those regions where separate Catholic cemeteries are not allowed, then the procedure must be as follows: When the part reserved to Catholics is to be blessed, a certain extreme portion should be left without any blessing, divided into two sections, one for the unbaptised infants, the other for the non-Catholics and others who have been denied.[32]

26 C. 12, XIII, 28; Cavagnis, l. c., No. 283.
27 Can. 1212.
28 See Section III, page .
29 Blat, l. c., No. 66.
30 Acta et Decreta, Tit. XIII, No. 602.
31 Can. 1212.
32 Coronata, l. c., No. 141.

CHAPTER IX. CARE OF THE CEMETERY

1. Enclosure

The nature of sacred places demands that they be kept in as befitting a manner as is deemed suitable for each one. In this wise, the New Code prescribes that every cemetery must be properly enclosed and carefully guarded.[1] The law does not specify as to what manner of enclosure would be most suitable. This should be left to the judgment of the ecclesiastical authorities in charge of the various cemeteries. A serviceable wall of stone would appear highly suitable. However, decent hedges or wire fences would not be out of place. The Third Plenary Council of Baltimore "gravely admonishes the rectors of churches of their incumbent obligation to preserve the cemeteries in a fit and decent condition, lest, from their unkempt or neglected appearance, the faithful have a just cause for complaint and be averse to their interment therein."[2]

2. Custody

In regards to the custody of the cemeteries, the wording of the New Code is clear—"cemeteries must be carefully guarded."[3] This prescription is to provide for the safe-keeping of these holy places, and to prevent any acts of depredation or violation taking place therein. In most places, the ecclesiastical authorities employ a keeper who resides in the vicinity and looks after the grounds. This seems to be what is meant here by the canon.

---

1 Can. 1210.

2 Acta et Decreta, No. 319.

3 Can. 1210.

3. Monuments

Catholic faith and piety demands that the tombstones and monuments be constructed and ornamented in a religious and befitting style. The law instructs the authorities in charge of the cemeteries who may be the parish priests—the Superior, in the case of private cemeteries—or even the Ordinary of the place, that they take necessary means to provide that the epitaphs, eulogies, and ornaments of the monuments be in harmony with the religious significance of the holy place. Anything not in harmony with Catholic faith and piety should not be tolerated. The rather prevalent custom in some places, of decorating the tombstones with vulgar statues of pagan deities and worldly maxims, may never, under any pretext whatsoever, be allowed to creep into our Catholic cemeteries. Emblems of masonic sects are expressly forbidden to be placed on the graves or stones.[4] The question was asked the S. Congregation of Rites regarding the installing of lights, electric lamps and the like in vaults and mausoleums. The answer was favorable inasmuch as these illuminations were conducive to the decent adornment of the tombs, and symbolic of the belief in the Resurrection of the Body.[5]

4. Mortuaries

In northern countries the severity of the winter season causes the ground to freeze very solidly and the digging of the graves is very arduous. Consequently mortuaries, ossuaries and the like, are built to serve for the temporary winter quarters of the bodies. The Council of Quebec prescribed that these buildings be adorned with sacred symbols with at least a crucifix in evidence, to denote the holy character of such a place.[6]

4 S. C. S. Off., 12 Dec., 1840=Coll. P. F., No. 1601.
5 30 Oct., 1922=A. A. S., Vol. XIV, p. 598.
6 Acta et Decreta, Tit. XIII, No. 601.

CHAPTER X. SPECIAL REGULATIONS CONCERNING CORPSES

1. Premature Burial

What could be dreaded more than hasty or careless burial before the certain fact of death has been ascertained? The Ritual expressly prescribes that no corpse is to be buried, and especially so in cases of sudden death, unless after a sufficient lapse of time so that there will be absolutely no room for doubt of the death. The New Code repeats the text of the Ritual.[1] In regards to certainty or proof of actual death, due caution must be exercised. Formerly, certain signs were considered as sufficient to establish decease, such as the ceasing of sensibility, of respiration, stopping of the pulse, etc. But it has been clearly demonstrated in more modern times that these are by no means sufficient indications that life has departed, and particularly in the case of sudden death. Persons have been known to revive and live after prolonged periods of apparent death, in trances when all animation seemed to be gone. One certain sign of death is decomposition of the body, i. e.—when the last vestige of life, cellular activity, desists. Special instructions were given to missionaries that they take every precaution against possible premature burial, and that, even in cases of necessity when time urges as in time of plagues, famine, etc., they must not allow burial before a proper interval of time has elapsed to remove all doubt of actual death.[2] This provision of the Ritual and also of the Code might appear superfluous to many. Most probably, it has been inserted for the notice of those who dwell where civil provision in such cases is lacking. In most places, civil laws and the coroner's inquest attends to these

1 Can. 1213; Roman Ritual, Tit. VI, C. 1, n. 3.
2 S. C. S. Off., 10 April, 1777=Coll. P. F., No. 521, n. 2.

matters, while the modern process of embalming, properly performed, will obviate any danger of burial of a living person.[3]

2. Exhumation

(1) *Sacredness of the Place*

The dominion of the Church over Catholic cemeteries and over the bodies of the dead who have been interred, is inviolable. Consequently in such a serious matter as this, no corpse which has been laid to rest by ecclesiastical burial, regardless of place or circumstance of burial, may be exhumed unless with the permission of the Ordinary.[4] If the laws of the State require its permission, surely one must not consider himself exempt from the required permission of the Ordinary.[5] This permission is not confined only to those Catholic cemeteries, properly so-called, with which the State in no wise interferes; but also is it required in the case of municipal or common cemeteries. When Catholics are buried in these latter—either a portion is reserved to them and blessed—or at the very least, the single graves are blessed.[6] Consequently the grave is a sacred place and must not be disturbed unlawfully, for the Church is the quasi-custodian even of the bodies of the faithful. Such is denoted by the employment of the word, "ubivis" in the text.[7] In some instances, the demands of the civil law might present serious difficulty to the application of this ecclesiastical requirement; such a difficulty would allow of the omission of this prescribed permission of the Ordinary.[8]

---

3 Coronata, l. c., No. 150; Augustine, l. c., p. 112.

4 Can. 1214, No. 1; Rit. Rom. Tit. VI, C. 1, No. 18; Wernz, l. c., No. 472; Ojetti, "Cadav," No. 672.

5 Coronata, l. c., No. 151, n. 4.

6 Can. 1206, Nos. 2, 3.

7 Can. 1214, No. 1.

8 Can. 1175.

(2) *Required Permission*

The New Code mentions only the Ordinary as the necessary authority to grant this permission. However, in regards to those private cemeteries of exempt Religious, the Major Superior of the Order could grant this required permission even in instances where laics had been interred in these cemeteries.[9] When the necessity of exhumation is grave and time urges, and when recourse to the Ordinary for his permission cannot be had, it would be lawful to presume his consent.[10]

(3) *Denial of Permission*

The Ordinary is directed to refuse this permission for exhumation, if the corpse referred to cannot be distinguished with certainty, from other corpses.[11] It is necessary to have sufficient proof and indication that such a one is the corpse specified. This law is of long standing.[12] It derives due importance especially when the concern is of those bodies of persons who had been denied ecclesiastical burial and who should never have been allowed interment in a sacred place. Then must parish priests and others of authority be very careful that these bodies can be distinguished with certainty from the other bodies, before the exhumation may commence.[13]

(4) *Provisory Interment*

If the corpse has been given provisory burial, the permission of the Ordinary would not be required for its exhumation and transfer to a cemetery for finished sepulture.[14] This happens frequently in time of war when bodies are buried hurriedly for the time being,

9 Coronata, No. 151, n. 3.
10 Coronata, No. 151, not. 4.
11 Can. 1214, No. 2.
12 C. 12, XIII, 28.
13 Coronata, l. c., No. 151, n. 7.
14 Can. 1214, No. 1.

and afterwards exhumed and transferred to suitable cemeteries. For this procedure it is evident that the permission of the Ordinary is not needed.

(5) *Anatomical Dissection*

May bodies be exhumed for purposes of scientific dissection? There is no ecclesiastical regulation prohibiting this. But, of course, it is clearly evident that the permission of the Ordinary must be first obtained and due precautions exercised that only the bodies concerned are disturbed. In murder cases, for instance, it is sometimes necessary to exhume corpses for the purpose of performing autopsies. Permission may also be granted to medical students to obtain certain corpses for dissection in their university laboratories. A general permission could be granted and exercised, providing that due caution and accuracy be employed in this delicate matter.[15]

---

15 Coronata, l. c., No. 151, n. 7.

SECTION II. FUNERAL SERVICES

In the third book of the New Code, the II and III chapters treat of ecclesiastical sepulture in the stricter sense, i. e.—the conveying of the body to the church, the funeral and burial services—and the granting or denying of such. Some authors, such as Schmalzgrueber, Reiffenstuel, Wernz, Devoti, Laurentius and others, have drawn a sharp division in their treatment, by placing "Cemeteries" under the general heading of "Sacred Places"—and "Ecclesiastical Sepulture" under the heading of "Sacramentals." Wernz proposes as a reason for this order—the order followed in the Roman Ritual. "Sepulture," according to his form, consists (1) in the Catholic rite or complexus of the sacred ceremonies, prayers and functions, (2) in the interment of the body in a sacred place.[1]

Nevertheless, the order employed by the New Code, whereby cemeteries and funeral services and the regulations concerning the grant or denial, are grouped in three chapters under the one title of "Ecclesiastical Sepulture;" and placed in the section "Sacred Places," is at once highly convenient and agreeable. This order has been observed in the preceding section of this treatise, and will be continued in the remaining two sections.

PART I

The Obligation of Funeral Services

The obligation of providing and obtaining the prescribed funeral rites, should be clearly evident to all. From the point of view of religion, this is, not only suitable and becoming, but really urgent. "The entire

1 Wernz, l. c., Tom. III, Pars. Secunda, Sectio II, Cap. II, Tit. XXXIII.

ceremony prescribed by the Church for the obsequies of the faithful is calculated to show respect for the body created to the image and likeness of God, the erstwhile temple of the Holy Ghost, and to reflect belief in those three consoling dogmas of the Communion of Saints, the Resurrection of the Body, and Life Everlasting.''[2] The recognition of this obligation has always been foremost in the history of the Church.[3] However, no explicit law has been codified prior to the New Code, relative to this detail.[4] Now, a special canon states, that, ''unless there is a weighty reason to the contrary, the bodies of the faithful, prior to the funeral, must be transferred from the place where they repose, to the church, where the funeral services—the complete order of ceremonies and functions, which are compiled in the approved liturgical books—shall be held.[5]

CHAPTER I. EXCUSING CAUSES

This obligation is a grave one, since only a grave cause may excuse from it. Circumstances of time, place, etc., may give rise to various reasons which will be of sufficient weight to excuse from this obligation. Serious plagues, danger in war-stricken regions, and the like, would remove this obligation. But such a reason as the danger of offending or antagonising people, cannot for an instant be entertained as a sufficiently grave cause.[1]

By this discipline the custom of burying the bodies of the faithful from their homes without bringing them to the church for the services, is reprobated by the first part of the canon, thus repeating the tenour of a decree

---

2 ''Parish Priests and Christian Burial''—Rev. J. H. Murphy.

3 C. 2, III, 12, in Vito, m, Schmalzgrueber, l. c., Tom. III, Tit. XXVIII, No. 6; Moulart, l. c., Cap. I, Art. II, page 138.

4 Coronata, l. c., No. 155.

5 Can. 1215.

---

1 Coronata, l. c., No. 156.

of the S. Congregation of Rites.[2] Yet, the strict obligating force of this canon seems to have been in some doubt when a question was sent to the "Pontifical Commission for the Authentic Interpretation of the Canons of the Code," asking whether the danger of offending certain persons ("malumore") would be sufficient to excuse from transferring the corpse to the church. The commission replied unconditionally in the negative and added, that any custom of non-transfer of the body to the church before burial, must be abolished.[3]

The Cardinal Archbishop of Rio Janeiro, sent the following question to the S. Congregation of Rites: "The rites of the exsequies as prescribed in the Roman Ritual, are not observed in this diocese because the remains are not brought to the church, on account of the civil laws which demand that burial take place within 24 hours after death; and moreover, because the cemeteries, which are subject to the civil law, are quite distant from the parishes. The parish priests are called to the house and there perform the services. Consequently, what rubrics and mode of action should be observed in this case?" The S. Congregation replied, "that the Ritual and the Canon Law must be observed whenever it can be done. (If the full ceremonial cannot be observed.) The family of the deceased must see to it, that, at least, there be a funeral service with corpse morally present, according to the rubrics and the decrees."[4] Thus such extraordinary contingencies are given due consideration by the law and allow of possible exceptions in specific cases.[5]

The formula of the funeral services in the Ritual is composed in three separate sections, the "levatio corporis," or services in the house of death and conveying the body to the church—the funeral services in the church—and the rites attendant upon the burial in

---

2 21 April, 1873, No. 3291.
3 16 Oct., 1919=A. A. S., Vol. XI, p. 479, sq.
4 28 Feb., 1920=A. A. S., Vol. XII, page 128.
5 Blat, l. c., No. 73.

the cemetery. In rural districts and especially in the large cities of the United States and Canada, where considerable distances, lack of time, frequency of funerals, and often the lack of sufficient priests render this service of the "levatio corporis" very inconvenient and frequently, impossible. Consequently the custom of omitting this part of the ceremony obtains for many dioceses.

By the burial services are designated only those prescribed by the Roman Ritual and thus all other ceremonies or rites are not allowed unless for serious reason, express permission has been granted for their toleration.

CHAPTER II. THOSE OBLIGED

1. The Faithful

The obligation incumbent on the faithful of employing the burial service may be estimated by the fact that every Catholic is expressly forbidden to ordain that the burial take place without the ecclesiastical services. "For, the will of the individual in this serious matter cannot conflict with the public law, which absolutely prescribes such for the faithful."[1] Consequently, even though one would have inserted in his last will, a clause to the effect that he abjures and forbids ecclesiastical sepulture for himself—the ecclesiastical superior and the relatives of this person should pay no attention to this clause, providing, of course, the person was otherwise worthy of ecclesiastical sepulture.[2]

2. Connections of the Deceased

The heirs, relatives and friends of the deceased should demand that he be given these holy rites. In no

1 Wernz, l. c., Tit. XXVIII, No. 780, Not. 35.
2 Ibidem.

wise may any perverse relative or friend refuse or impede ecclesiastical sepulture for the worthy deceased.

3. Priests

All the priests who have had the spiritual care of the deceased are certainly bound to see that he receives proper ecclesiastical sepulture. The necessary expenses for funeral services must not be used as a pretext for denying such to poor or destitute persons. The New Code does not clearly determine just what obligation is in force in this detail. However the Ritual states that the poor are to be given ecclesiastical sepulture gratis. And the parish priest or pious confraternities and associations—according to local custom, should bear the burden of the expenses.[3] If this matter of expense can be sustained as a grave cause excusing, then the obligation ceases. Yet, in the great majority of cases, the priests, having the care of such persons who have no means to pay for the expenses, are not excused from the entire order of the services. A portion may be omitted with sufficient reason—as local custom will decide.[4]

The Ritual prescribes that the entire order of the funeral services, "Exequiarum Ordo," be followed, even to the grave.[5] A reasonable cause will suffice to excuse from part. In the case of lack of time, a portion of the services especially of the Office of the Dead, may be omitted; and if there is little time available, this office may be omitted entirely, but the remaining prayers must be said. In many countries custom has sanctioned the omission of this part of the service, as is noticeable in America today, except of course, for the funeral services of priests.

In regard to those persons dying in public hospitals, refuges and the like—the burden of the expense can hardly be imposed upon the priest in charge of this

---

3 Tit. VI, C. 1, n. 8.
4 Coronata, l. c., No. 159.
5 Tit. VI, C. 3.

institution. In such cases, keeping Canon 1235 #2 in mind, these destitutes are to buried gratis with such funeral exequies as the local custom will determine.[6]

At one time there existed doubt as to the admissibility of the ecclesiastical rites when the corpse was conveyed to and from the church in a vehicle. A decree of the S. Congregation of Rites decided that this does not interfere at all with the seemliness of the function.[7] Thus, there can be no objection to the modern, "automobile funerals."

PART II

The Church of the Funeral

To facilitate matters, the law prescribes regulations for practise to follow in regards to the proper church of the funeral services. The church of the funeral is that church to which the body of the deceased must be brought, according to law, for the services.[1]

CHAPTER I. DESIGNATION

It must be noted that there are various and special regulations governing the lawful designation of the church of the funeral. Not all churches may fulfill this office, legitimately and agreeably. Very often the designation has been made by the person before dying. However, such determination is regulated by choice—privilege—special law—or by reason of domicile in a parish.

---

6 Coronata, l. c., No. 158.
7 5 March, 1872, No. 3212.

---

1 Coronata, l. c., No. 161.

CHAPTER II. THE ORDER TO BE OBSERVED

The following order is to be followed in deciding what church can be lawfully designated for the funeral services.

1. Selection

One is free to select any church. The same applies to those churches to which are attached ancestral or private cemeteries. Before the New Code, the rights of ancestral tombs (sepulchra majorum seu gentilitium), were recognized with every consideration. In fact, the Decretals of Gregory IX stress the importance and advisability of this style of sepulture by calling attention to that prevalent attitude on the part of the Israelites who invariably sought interment in the "tombs of their fathers."[1] This is not quite the case under the New Code. Rather are parochial rights stressed and placed in precedence, as one notices from the very first canon dealing with this matter.[2] Still, no obligation at all is imposed. Perfect freedom is left to each one to select whatever church he may desire, with a few exceptions as are treated in Canons 1223-1226, which matters will be discussed at length when treating of these canons.

2. Parish Church

The parish church of the deceased is the first one to be considered in relation to this matter of funeral services. Providing that no other church had been selected by the deceased, and no right obtains by reason of special law—privilege—or other domiciles—then the proper church of the funeral services is the parish church of the deceased. Again, it must be remembered that, if the deceased had a title to ancestral tombs, etc., such must

1 C. 1, X, 28, III; Schmalzgrueber, l. c., Tit. XXVIII, No. 27, sq.
2 Canon 1216.

be respected, even though he had not designated any church.[3]

3. Ancestral Title

Certain persons may legitimately enjoy the right of interment in ancestral plots or tombs. Such persons are free to designate them. In such cases, even though one had not made any designation, the body is to be transferred to that cemetery, if such is convenient; while the church to which this cemetery is attached, acquires the right to the funeral. In the case of such "sepulchra majorum seu gentilitium" being situated in a common civil cemetery, then the proper church, providing none such have already been chosen, is designated by common or special law as the instance may require.[4] More of this later.

CHAPTER III. REGULATION OF THE DESIGNATION

1. Common Law

The common law regarding the church of the funeral, is, "that the body is to be brought to the parish church of the deceased."[1] In this very canon an exception to the common law is made whereby this law does not bind if the deceased had selected a church other than his parish church. Several contingencies and even difficulties can arise with various existing circumstances, and these shall be treated singly.

3 Canon 1229, No. 1.
4 Canon 1229; Coronata, l. c., No. 163.

1 Can. 1216, No. 1; C. 24, XV, 33; C. 2, 2, III, 12, in Vito, m, Reiff., Tit. XXVIII.

(1) *Providing Death Occurred in the Parish of the Deceased*

Then, the general principle of Canon 1216 is to be observed when such is not obstructed by elective or ancestral sepulture.[2]

a. The Proper Parish

Each one belongs to a parish by reason of:

(a) Title of domicile—One may belong to a parish by reason of title of domicile in a parish or quasi-parish.[3] Domicile is acquired by ten years' residence, or by any period of residence providing that one had the intention of remaining there perpetually.[4]

(b) Title of quasi-domicile—One may belong to a parish by reason of title of quasi-domicile in a parish or quasi-parish. This is acquired by protracted residence or more than six months, or by any length of stay, providing that one had the intention of remaining there for the greater part of a year.[5]

(c) Lack of title—If one has neither a domicile or a quasi-domicile in any parish, then the proper parish of such a one is that in which he actually lived.[6]

(d) Domicile of origin—The domicile of one's origin has no force in this matter of funeral services. The domicile must be either, voluntary as regulated by the foregoing canons—or necessary, such as the domicile of the husband is the domicile for the wife.[7] Note however, in this last case, that such interferes in no way with the right of election.

(e) Lack of parish—It may happen in missionary countries that one might die where there was no parish or quasi-parish. In such a case the church of the funeral

---

2 C. 3, III, 12, in Vito; Schmalzgrueber, l. c., Tit. XXVIII, No. 39; Lauren, No. 939.

3 Can. 94, No. 1.

4 Can. 92, No. 1.

5 Can. 92, No. 2.

6 Can. 94, No. 2.

7 Maroto, "Institutiones Juris Canonici," Tom. I, No. 410; Coronata, l. c., No. 164.

would be that one closest at hand. Likewise, when one dies on board ship, the chaplain of this ship would look after the funeral services.

(f) Diocesan domicile—If one had a domicile in a diocese but possessed no domicile whatsoever in any parish, then the church of the funeral would be that one of the parish in which the person died.[8]

b. Several Parishes

The New Code states that if the deceased belonged to several parishes, then the church of the funeral is that church of the parish in which he had died.[9] This ruling was not definitely established in the past.[10] In fact, one opinion held, that in such a case, the church of the funeral would be that one which the deceased was accustomed to attend.[11] But the more general opinion held that the church of the funeral in this case was the church of the parish where death occurred.[12] Note that this canon refers to correct and lawful attachment to these parishes—not mere choice of a certain parish or title to an ancestral tomb in another parish.[13]

One may belong to several parishes, in the following ways:

1. By possessing a real domicile in one parish and a quasi-domicile in another.
2. By possessing a necessary domicile in one parish, and a quasi-domicile in another.
3. By possessing several domiciles or quasi-domiciles.

A pertinent decision was given by the S. Congregation of Rites.[14] A family had a domicile in a city parish, A. The wife lived at this family's summer villa for about

---

8 Can. 94, No. 3.

9 Can. 1216, No. 2.

10 C. w. III, 12, in Vito.

11 Schmalzgrueber, l. c., Tit. XXVIII, No. 48; Ferraris, "Sepult.," No. 24; Moulart, p. 191, No. 2143.

12 Ferraris, l. c., "Sepult.," No. 25; Moulart, l. c., p. 191; Ojetti, "Exequiae D'Angelo," l. c., p. 89.

13 Coronata, l. c., No. 165.

14 12 March, 1881=A. S. Sedis, Vol. XIV, p. 209.

eight months of each year. She died in this second parish, B; and the parish priest performed the funeral services. The S. Congregation decided that the pastor of parish B, was entitled to hold the funeral. Such is the tenour of the New Code.[15] So that, any person, having a domicile in one parish and a quasi-domicile in another and dying in this latter, then the parish where the death occurred, is the legitimate one for the funeral services. Because the pastor of the parish in which one had a quasi-domicile is a perfectly lawful pastor of the deceased.[16]

c. In Doubt

Doubt may arise concerning the rights of other churches to the funeral services. In such cases, the principle of Canon Law must be observed, namely, "the right of one's parish church must always prevail."[17] Such doubt may arise between:

(a) The parish church of the deceased and a church of election. If there is doubt as to whether the deceased had really chosen another church for the services, then the presumption of the law is always in favor of the parish church.

(b) The parish church of the deceased and the church pertaining to the ancestral tomb. The same rule is to be applied.

(c) If doubt arises concerning the several parishes in which the deceased had domiciles—then Canons 1216 #2 and 1218, are to be applied. These two canons are treated in detail elsewhere.

N. B.=To apply this principle, it must be understood that a reasonable doubt exists—that the rights of another church are not minimized or discriminated against. If it can be shown that another church has legitimate claims then no preference may be shown for the parish church.

---

15 Can. 1216, No. 2.
16 Moulart, l. c., p. 191; Many, l. c., No. 172.
17 Can. 1217.

(2) *When Death Occurred Outside the Parish of the Deceased*

a. First part of Canon 1218

(a) Tenour of the canon—The New Code proposes a general rule to follow, "that when death occurred outside one's own parish, the body is to be brought for the funeral services, to the parish church of the deceased which is the nearest, when it can be conveniently carried there on foot; otherwise it is to be brought to the church of the parish in which death occurred."[18] There seems to be a stressing of a less probable and rather rare situation by the Code in this paragraph of Canon 1218. The preceding canons have treated distinctly of the rights of parishes. At first glance, one is inclined to remark—why then limit this important right by a mathematical scale of distance to be determined by the laws of pedestrianism? Really, the only practical effect of this paragraph is that it shows a direction to follow in the case of persons, who have died outside their parish and who have no relatives or friends who will see to their interment; and this ruling has a bearing on the parochial right to the stipend—which will be discussed later. In such cases, the body is to be brought to the parish church only if this conveying can be conveniently made on foot; otherwise the same rule as in Canon 1216 #2, is to be followed.[19] Because in the majority of cases, relatives and friends of the deceased attend to the funeral arrangements; and of course, the Code allows them every freedom.

(b) Effect of the canon—This paragraph of the canon deals only with persons who belong to a parish by reason of domicile or quasi-domicile, and also with those persons who had elected no church, and had no title to ancestral plots. If one had belonged to several parishes and died afar, the corpse is to be brought to that parish which is nearest. Following the rules of

---

18 Can. 1218, No. 1; C. 2, III, 12, in Vito.
19 D'Angelo, l. c., p. 100.

grammar, the relative pronoun "quae" in this first part of the canon, refers to "paroeciae"—not to "ecclesiam." Consequently, even—as may easily happen in large cities—though a church of another parish may be nearer to the place of the death, the correct parish for the funeral is that one to which one had belonged and is relatively nearer than his other parishes, even though it be quite distant from the place of death.

N. B.=In the old law, this prescription, as it is stated in Canon 1218 #1, had a much greater significance than it enjoys nowadays, especially in America. Transportation of the body to the parish church, if this took a day's journey on foot, was looked upon by canonists as dangerous.[20] In our times, automobiles and other modern conveniences render this contingency unnecessary: consequently, this discipline has little value.[21]

b. The Second Part of Canon 1218

(a) Directions for the Ordinary—Here the Ordinary is directed to determine, after examining the special circumstances—the distance—and other details which would be inconvenient for the conveying of the body to the church, or to the place of burial. This estimate on the part of the Ordinary would be done, most preferably, at a synod and by means of the diocesan statutes, following the prescriptions demanded by the first part of the canon.[22]

(b) Different dioceses—If the deceased belonged to several parishes of different dioceses—then the diocesan statutes designated by the Ordinary of the diocese where death occurred, would obtain.

(c) Persons concerned—Again it is to be noted that this designation or norm of procedure on the part of the Ordinary as prescribed by this canon, is concerned only with those persons who die and have no one interested in them to look after their funeral arrange-

---

20 Ojetti, l. c., "Exequiae," No. 2143.
21 C. 1, III, 6, Extrav. Commun.
22 Coronata, l. c., No. 168; Augustine, l. c., p. 120.

ments. And in such cases, it would be the duty of the pastor of the deceased to look after the funeral arrangements, having notified the pastor of the place where death took place; providing that the first paragraph of this canon be observed.

c. The Third Part of Canon 1218

"Even though the transferring to the church of the funeral or to the cemetery be quite convenient, the right is always allowed the family, heirs, or other interested persons to take charge of these details, providing that they assume the burden of the necessary expenses."[23]

(a) Liberty allowed—By this statement perfect liberty is left to the family and others to convey the body, not only to the parish church of the deceased—but likewise to an elected church or to an ancestral sepulture, as the case may be.[24]

(b) Several parishes—If the deceased had belonged to several parishes, had not chosen any special church, had no right to ancestral title, and died afar—it is apparent that the relatives and friends have every right to remove the body to one of these parishes, which they themselves decide upon.

(c) Rights of the pastor—After such transfer of the body, the pastor of the church to which the body has been brought, has the right to look after the usual arrangements—not the pastor of the parish in which death occurred. However, this first pastor should notify the second priest of this affair.[25]

(d) Persons concerned—Those persons to whom the New Code grants the freedom of taking charge of the funeral arrangements, are not only the family, heirs and close relatives—but also friends, confraternities, municipalities, lawful fraternal societies and the like. Such is clearly evident from the words—"aliisve quorum interest."

---

23 Can. 1218, No. 3.
24 Can. 1221, No. 2; Can. 1229.
25 Can. 1230, No. 2.

(e) Local custom—Possibly customs exist in some places which suggest different procedure than that of this canon. If such customs are legitimate, they should not be interfered with—as the New Code here inserts no reproving or cancelling clauses to that effect.[26]

N. B.=It must always be borne in mind, when concerned with the above details, that it has been presupposed that death has occurred outside one's parish.

2. Special Law

Although it is a general principle that persons may select a church for their funeral services, nevertheless the law of the Church has legislated in a special manner for certain classes.

(1) *Roman Pontiff*

The New Code makes no mention of the "ecclesia funerandi" of the Roman Pontiff. Some legislation on this matter is contained in the Constitution of Pius X "Vacante Sede."[27]

a. Ordinarily, the Church of the funeral and interment of the Roman Pontiff is the Vatican Basilica.[28]

b. If death occurred outside of Rome—which would very rarely occur in modern times—and the body could not be brought to the Holy City, then interment would take place in the principal church of that place.[29]

c. If death took place in the city, and the Roman Pontiff had chosen a special church for the interment, the body is to be brought to the Vatican Basilica for the prescribed ceremonies of the exequies, and afterwards transferred to the other church for interment.[30]

---

26 Coronata, l. c., No. 169.

27 25 Dec., 1904=This document is contained in an appendix to the Code.

28 Ferraris, l. c., "Sepult.," No. 57; Moulart, l. c., p. 195; Many, l. c., No. 173; Coron., No. 1.

29 Ferraris, l. c., No. 58; Moulart, l. c., p. 195; Many, l. c., No. 173; Coronata, Nos. 172, 173.

30 Ferraris, l. c., No. 59; Coronata, l. c., No. 172.

(2) *Cardinals*

a. Providing that the Cardinal had not selected a special church for his funeral services:

(a) If the Cardinal had died in Rome, his body is to be brought for the services, to the church which the Roman Pontiff will have designated.[31]

(b) If the Roman Pontiff did not designate a church, or if such designation was obstructed, or if the Holy See was vacant, then the proper church of the funeral, according to one opinion—would be the church of the Title of the Cardinal, and according to another opinion the proper church would be the parochial church of the Cardinal's domicile.[32]

(c) If the Cardinal had died outside of Rome, then the church of the funeral will be that more prominent church of the place.[33]

(d) If the Cardinal was a residential Bishop, then the body must be brought to the cathedral church, if this can be done conveniently; if not, then to the more prominent church of the city or place.[34]

b. If the Cardinal had designated a special church for his funeral services, this wish must be respected and attended to. The same applies to any title to an ancestral sepulture.[35]

(3) *Bishops*

a. Bishops may designate any special church for their funeral services.

b. If they had not chosen any special church:

(a) If such can be done conveniently, the body of a residential Bishop must be brought to the cathedral church.[36]

---

31 Canon 1219, No. 1.

32 Ferraris, l. c., No. 60; Many, l. c., No. 176; Coronata, l. c., 173; Wernz, l. c., No. 775.

33 Can. 1219, No. 1; Moulart, l. c., p. 195.

34 Can. 1219, No. 2; Coronata, l. c., No. 173.

35 Ferraris, l. c., No. 60; Many, l. c., No. 176; Coronata, l. c., No. 173.

36 Can. 1219, No. 2.

(b) If this be inconvenient, then the body is to be brought to the more prominent church of the city or town.

(c) The same procedure is to be followed in the case of any residential Bishop, whether he be a Cardinal, Abbot or Prelate nullius.[37] Likewise in the case of a Prefect or Vicar Apostolic.[38]

(d) Even though death had occurred outside his diocese, the body of the Bishop should be brought to the cathedral church, unless this would be very inconvenient—"si incommode." Otherwise, the same rule is to be applied as in (b).

(e) It seems more probable, that in the case of residential Bishops, the funeral services should be held in the cathedral church in preference to ancestral title of sepulture. There is—or rather was, an opinion which gives preference to "sepulchra majorum" over the cathedral church.[39] If death took place outside the diocese, and transfer of the body to the cathedral church would be very inconvenient, then these "sepulchra majorum" would have an equal significance with the "ecclesia insignior" of that place.[40]

(f) If the Bishop had charge of two diocese united equally under his office, then the church of the funeral would be the cathedral church of the diocese in which he died. If these united diocese were not on an equal standing—one with the other, then the church of the funeral would be that cathedral church of the more prominent diocese, unless of course, a transfer to this church would be highly inconvenient.[41]

(g) Titular Bishops, unless they are Papal Nuncios or Legates—by common and ordinary law are to be brought to the church of their proper parish, with the exception for right to election, ancestral title, or unless transportation would be very inconvenient—when in such

---

37 Can. 1219, No. 2.
38 Can. 294, No. 1.
39 Ferraris, l. c., "Sepult.," No. 66.
40 Many, l. c., No. 174; Coronata, l. c., No. 174, 2'.
41 Ferraris, l. c., No. 66; Coronata, l. c., No. 174, 6'.

a case, the church of the funeral would be that one of the place where death occurred.[42]

(4) *Priests*

A general ruling of the New Code states that the church of the funeral for residential beneficiaries, is the church of their benefice unless they have selected another.[43]

a. Canons of the Cathedral Chapter—A legitimate custom may provide that the church of the funeral for these priests be the cathedral, otherwise the church would be that of their benefice.[44]

b. Canons of a Collegiate Chapter—The church of their benefice should be the funeral church, although a legitimate custom may provide otherwise.[45]

c. Parish Priests—In practically all countries the parish priests have benefices and consequently, for them the proper funeral church would be that one where they had their residence.[46]

d. Simple Priests—Vicars, curates and assistant priests have no special signification in this matter. They come under the common law with the faithful. Consequently the church of their funeral services would be their parish church.[47]

e. Non-residential Beneficiaries—These enjoy no special provisions of the law, but are treated as above in (d).[48]

(5) *Religious*

The following regulations refer to all Religious in the canonical sense—not to those who lead a Religious life in community without vows as are described in

42 Canon 1220.

43 Can. 1220.

44 Ferraris, l. c., "Canonicae," No. 11, sq.; Many, l. c., No. 177; Coronata, No. 175.

45 Many, l. c., No. 178; Coronata, l. c., No. 175, 2'.

46 Reiffenstuel, l. c., Tit. XXVIII, No. 14; Many, l. c., No. 179; Coronata, l. c., No. 175.

47 Reiffenstuel, l. c., Tit. XXVIII, Nos. 13, 15; Many, l. c., No. 179; Coronata, No. 175.

48 Many, l. c., No. 179; Coronata, l. c., No. 175, d.

Canon 673. In case that one is inclined to apply here Canon 490—which states that the term, "Religiosi," even though in the masculine gender, refers to female Religious also, unless the context or nature of the law prove the contrary—it is more suitable for the sake of clarity and order, to apply the following rules and observations to male Religious exclusively. Female Religious are treated in another paragraph—(8), where all their special regulations and privileges are discussed. (Some of these rules of Canon 1221, however are applicable to female Religious.)

a. Church of the Religious—The bodies of professed Religious must be brought for the funeral services to the church or oratory of their House or, at least, to their Institute.[49] Formerly, this prescription applied only to Regulars, strictly so-called.[50] At present, the law in using this term "religiosi" extends this to all males who in any Order or Congregation—even one of Diocesan Institution—have made at least a temporary profession.[51]

b. Superiors—By this law are bound also the Superior of the Religious of whatever rank or dignity, with the exception of Bishops.[52] However the Code makes special provision in the case of Abbots or Prelates Nullius.[53]

c. Professed Religious and Novices—Professed Religious are not permitted to exercise any privilege of elective sepulture.[54] Novices, however, may do so.[55] Formerly, when the Religious was a long way from his House, he could then select a special church for his funeral services.[56] This is no longer permitted: only Novices may choose such.

---

49 Can. 1221.
50 C. 16, XV, 31; C. 5, III, 12, in Vito; Many, l. c., No. 180.
51 Coronata, l. c., No. 176, a.
52 Can. 1224, 2'.
53 Can. 1219, No. 2.
54 Can. 1224, 2'.
55 Can. 1221, No. 1.
56 C. 5, III, 12, in Vito.

d. Death in a distant place—If a Religious should die in a place so far distant so that the body cannot be conveniently conveyed to a church of his House or Order, the funeral service is to be held in the church of the parish where he died.[57] This is given only to serve as an excuse from the aforegoing law. If the expenses of transportation would be defrayed by the order, or other persons, there is nothing to prevent the transportation to the House.[58]

e. Secularized Religious—Since they are freed from their vows and privileges, secularized Religious do not come under this ruling, but are subject to the common and ordinary law. The same applies for ejected or dismissed Religious.[59]

f. Exclaustrated Religious—Since they are not relieved of their vows, exclaustrated Religious retain the obligations of their profession and are not excepted from this ruling.[60] The same applies for apostate or fugitive Religious as such, for they are not freed and are still bound by the rules and vows of their Order. This obligation, of course, ceases with the cessation of their obligations in Religious profession.[61]

g. Exiled Religious—Religious who have been unlawfully suppressed and dispersed or exiled by civil statute, come under the common law and parochial jurisdiction—unless they have again formed a community of at least three, under their own Superior.[62]

h. Servants in a Religious House—The following observations apply only to servants in a House of male Religious.[63]

(a) Servants participate in these privileges of the Religious, providing that the two conditions be fulfilled, namely—that they are actually serving the Religious—

---

57 Can. 1221, No. 2.
58 Ferraris, l. c., No. 39; Coronata, l. c., No. 176.
59 Ferraris, l. c., No. 47; Many, l. c., No. 180.
60 Can. 638.
61 Coronata, l. c., No. 176.
62 Coronata, l. c., No. 176, i.
63 Coronata, l. c., No. 179, b.

and live within the precincts of the House.[64] Consequently, if either condition was lacking, this privilege ceases. If the servant boarded outside the House, or if one worked without being hired or employed, such a one would not be entitled.[65]

(b) The servants enjoy these privileges in the same way as the Novices, with the following exceptions and differences. If the servant died outside the House, the church of his funeral would be that one designated by common law—the parish church: while, in the case of a Novice having died outside the House, the body could then be brought to the House for funeral services.[66]

(c) The New Code inserts the term "stabiliter" which denotes that this habitation of the servant in the Religious House was permanent, if not in actual fact, at least in intention, as in the case of domicile.[67]

(6) *Guests, Students and Patients of Religious*

a. Unless there is evidence of a particular law or privilege, those who have died in a Religious House, even though this belongs to Regulars—or even though this is a college where they have resided as students—or even though this is a hospital where they have resided as guests or patients—they are governed by the rules of common law in regards to their funeral services as stated in Canons 1216-1218.[68]

b. Note that a particular obligation or right can be acquired by prescription or custom—while a privilege is acquired by real concession, besides by acquisition through prescription or through legitimate custom.[69] All Religious therefore, who can claim neither a particular law, nor a privilege, must permit the pastor in whose parish this House is located, to perform the funeral services in this case. The Barnabites were granted a

64 Can. 1221, No. 3; Conc. Trid. Sess. 24, C. 11; Sess. 25, C. 11.
65 Coronata, l. c., No. 179, e; Augustine, l. c., p. 124.
66 Can. 1221, No. 2.
67 Coronata, l. c., No. 179, d.
68 Can. 1222.
69 Wernz, l. c., Tom. I, No. 160; Can. 62.

privilege permitting their guests and all who died suddenly in their houses or colleges, to be buried by those Religious.[70]

c. The Bishop can grant a privilege exempting these persons from the common law, or parochial jurisdiction in this matter.[71]

d. In regards to the funeral services of those having died in hospitals, such is to be determined by common law. Note that a protracted sickness in the hospital for over six months would constitute a quasi-domicile in the parish where the hospital is located. Of course, exemption by reason of particular law or privilege, would apply here also.[72]

(7) *Seminarians*

a. The Rector of a Seminary exercises the office of pastor towards all who live in the Seminary.[73] And consequently, the church or oratory of the Seminary is their parish church. All who die in the Seminary therefore, are to be buried from this church. Of course, the right to elective sepulture and ancestral title, is understood.

b. There is a difference here between ordinary parochial rights, and the rights of a Seminary parish; and for this reason, Seminarians and those living in the Seminary, are governed by special law. This special law applies only when death has occurred in the Seminary.[74] If death took place outside the Seminary, the body is not to be transferred to the Seminary for funeral services.[75]

c. By the words, "illos qui in Seminario moriuntur," not only are the Seminarians themselves meant—but also are included the servants, professors, prefects, Sisters in charge of the domestic department, and the

70 Augustine, l. c., page 125.

71 Wernz, l. c., Tom. II, No. 828; Many, l. c., No. 164; Coronata, l. c., No. 181, d.

72 Coronata, l. c., No. 184.

73 Can. 1368.

74 Can. 1222.

75 Coronata, l. c., No. 185.

like.[76] If the Rector himself, die in the Seminary the proper church for the funeral is the Seminary chapel.[77]

(8) *Sisters*

a. Distinctions—Canon Law draws a distinction between, "Sorores"—Religious women who have taken only simple vows—and "Moniales"—who have taken solemn vows, or whose vows are by their rule solemn, but which have for certain countries been declared simple by order of the Holy See.[78]

b. Proper church—This distinction is retained in the matter of the proper church for the funeral of Sisters.

(a) "Moniales"—Whether they die within or away from their house, the "Moniales" are to be brought to the church or oratory of their house or institute. If such transportation is very inconvenient and no one will defray the necessary expenses, then the church of the funeral will be that of the parish where the death occurred. Thus it is noticed that "Moniales" enjoy all the privileges and special laws granted to "Religiosi."[79]

(b) Sorores"—They are divided into two classes, in the matter of regulating the proper church for their funeral services. The first class—are those Sisters (with simple vows) who have been exempt from parochial jurisdiction. Then the proper church of the funeral, whether death occurred in the house or elsewhere, would be that of the "moniales."[80] The Bishop can grant this concession of exemption.[81] The second class—are those Sisters (with simple vows) who have not obtained exemption from parochial jurisdiction. The proper church of the funeral for this class, whether death occurred in the house or elsewhere, in the parish church, and the regulations of common law are to be observed.[82]

76 Can. 1222.
77 Coronata, l. c., No. 185.
78 Can. 488, No. 7.
79 Cans. 490, 1221, No. 2, 1218, 1230, No. 5; Many, l. c., 186; Coronata, l. c., No. 177.
80 Can. 1230, No. 5; Wernz, l. c., 778, not. 32; Many, l. c., No. 187.
81 Can. 464, No. 2; Coronata, l. c., No. 177, not. 1,
82 Can. 1230, No. 5.

N. B.=On account of this distinction just discussed, it was thought more suitable to treat "Sisters" separately from "Religious," although this latter distinction is the only speciality which deprives all Sisters from being included in the regulations treating of Religious in Canon 1221.

3. The Church of Election

Under this heading will be discussed the regulations regarding elective sepulture, in the somewhat restrictive sense, i. e.—referring only to election of the church of the funeral. For several reasons, the church has drawn a sharp distinction between the election of the church of the funeral and the election of the cemetery. That of the cemetery will be treated in Part IV.

A. Former Legislation

The existing law as stated in the New Code is practically a repetition of the former discipline which has suffered very few alterations in its inception. In the Decretals of Gregory IX, this freedom of election is not only permitted, but enjoined on all.[83] Each one is his own lord and master in the selection of his own place of sepulture.[84] This freedom of choice is to enjoy every protection.[85] Any restriction of this privilege is not to be tolerated.[86] In the Decretal of Boniface VIII, election of sepulture is entirely independent of any obligation of domicile.[87] This is repeated in substance and clearly expounded in the Constitution of Clement V, and in the "Extravagantes Communes."[88] With some few minor changes, the New Code embodies the content of the former legislation.

---

83 C. 3, XIII, 28.
84 Schmalzgrueber, l. c., Tit. XXVIII, No. 10, sq.
85 C. 3, XIII, 28.
86 C. 6, XIII, 28.
87 C. 2, 4, III, 12, in Vito.
88 C. 2, III, in Clem.; C. 1, II, 1, in Extrav. Commun.; C. 1, 2, III, 6, in Extrav. Commun.

B. Present Legislation

(1) *Those Allowed Election*

All may choose their funeral church, unless they are expressly prohibited by law.[89] This canon makes special mention of wives and children of the age of puberty being included in this privilege. They are immune from any restriction of the husband or parents in this matter of election of the church.[90]

(2) *Those Prohibited Election*

a. "Impuberes"—Children who have not attained puberty are not allowed to choose.[91] For boys, the canonical age demanded, is—that they have completed their fourteenth year. For girls—they must have completed their twelfth year.[92] The New Code seems to imply that even after the death of the parents, the guardians are allowed to select the church of the funeral for the "impuberes."[93] In this wise—the father takes precedence in this matter of choosing; in defect of father, then the mother; then in defect of both parents, the guardians, uncles and aunts.[94]

b. Religious—Professed Religious of whatever rank or dignity except Bishops, are not permitted this right of choosing their funeral church.[95]

(a) The New Code binds all professed Religious by this restriction. Formerly, Religious with solemn vows, providing they retained their, "velle et nolle," were permitted to enjoy freedom of election.[96] And a special concession was formerly allowed in favor of major

---

89 Can. 1223, No. 1.

90 Can. 1223, No. 3; C. 3, C. XIII, q. 2; Reiffenstuel, l. c., Tit. XXVIII, No. 39.

91 Reiffenstuel, l. c., Tit. XXVIII, No. 41; Ojetti, l. c., "Exequiae," No. 2144.

92 Can. 88, No. 2.

93 Can. 1224, No. 1.

94 Devoti, l. c., page 546; Coronata, l. c., No. 191.

95 Can. 1224, 2'; C. 7, 10, XIII, 28; C. 4, 5, 888, 12, in Vito.

96 Ojetti, l. c., "Exequiae," No. 2144.

superiors and even regulars who died afar.[97] The reason for these extensions was deduced from the Decretal of Boniface VIII which contained—"Religious, unless they died at a remote distance from their proper monasteries, may not choose their sepulture when they have not the 'velle et nolle.' "[98] However, the New Code in its comprehensive statement allows of no exception to this rule in the case of professed Religious.[99] Even though the election had been made prior to Religious profession, such would not affect this general restriction.[100] In using the term, "Religiosi" it is evident that the Code employs it in the broad sense of Canon 490; consequently, not only male Religious, but also female Religious are included in this prohibition. Of course, it is understood that this prohibition does not bind novices.

(b) If the Religious was a Bishop, and a fortiori, if he was a Cardinal, this prohibition would not hold.[101] And, since the canon speaks of "episcopi" simply, they are also included Titular Bishops, Vicars and prefects Apostolic.[102]

(c) By perpetual secularization, a Religious is released from all the rules and regulations of his Order.[103] Consequently, this prohibition would not apply.[104] But in the case of only exclaustration such persons would not remain free to choose, because one still remains a Religious.[105]

(d) Ejected or dismissed Religious are ipso facto solved from the vows of Religion and consequently are not bound by this restriction. On the other hand, however, this is not to be applied to apostate or fugitive

---

97 Ferraris, l. c., "Sepult.," No. 39, sq.; Many, l. c., No. 164; Ojetti, l. c., No. 2144.

98 C. 5, III, 12, in Vito, Devoti, l. c., page 546, No. IV.

99 Coronata, l. c., No. 191 (Can. 1224).

100 Ibidem.

101 Canon 1224, 2'.

102 Reiffenstuel, l. c., Tit. XXVIII, No. 42; D'Angelo, l. c., page 57; Coronata, l. c., 191.

103 Canons 638, 640.

104 D'Angelo, l. c., page 57.

105 Can. 639.

Religious for they, "are not released from their vows or the obligations of their rule."[106]

c. "Indigni"—It is evident that those who are expressly denied ecclesiastical sepulture certainly are not free to select the church of their funeral. More of this later.

d. Insane persons—They who lack the use of reason are "de facto" excluded from freedom of election.[107]

(3) *The Liberty of this Election*

Preserving the traditional attitude in regards to that freedom of election of the funeral church, which the law of the church has always advocated and safeguarded, the New Code embodies a series of canons dealing with this aspect and expressly warns certain classes of persons from interfering—much less hindering—with the liberty of those who are allowed election of the funeral church or cemetery.

a. Taking the text substantially from the Decretals, the New Code states that all Religious and secular clergy are strictly forbidden to induce any person to vow, or swear, or in any way promise to choose their church for the funeral or their cemetery for the burial, or in any way to change his choice; but if such an inducement was made, the selection or change would be null and void.[108]

b. "Religiosi et clerici saeculares"—This canonical prohibition refers to all religious and all secular clerics. On the other hand, it does not refer to laics. The term "Religiosi," consequently is understood as affecting all male and female Religious.[109]

c. "Districte vetantur"—These words imply a severe and grave prohibition.

(a) In the old law, several penalties could be incurred by those disobeying this law, namely—nullity

---

106 Canons 645, 648.

107 Canons 88, 103, No. 1; D'Angelo, l. c., page 56.

108 Can. 1227.

109 Can. 490; Ferraris, l. c., "Sepult.," No. 123; Moulart, l. c., page 166; Many, l. c., No. 165; Coronata, l. c., No. 192, 7'.

of election; incapacity of electing another; and if sepulture followed, the Religious and clerics inducing such, were obliged to restore within ten days, all the offerings received and even the corpse itself if such were demanded. Religious who were contumacious in this matter, incurred "ipso facto" an interdict of their churches and cemeteries.[110] This censure, however, lapsed with its non-renewal in the constitution, "Apostolicae Sedis."[111] Likewise, a censure ipso facto incurred by those persons, added by Clement V was not renewed in this Constitution of Pius IX.[112]

(b) Under the New Code, no penalties are incurred by disobedience of this prohibition. The only result is that such election is rendered null and void. Of course, the Bishop could inflict penalties on such clerics who have committed this offense.

c. "Ad vovendum, jurandum, etc."—The designated persons are forbidden to induce one to vow, swear, pledge his word, or otherwise promise such election. These words are to be taken literally and strictly.[113] Consequently, a mere persuasion, or inducement without entailing any sort of promise, is not prohibited by this canon, and such election would be valid.[114]

d. "Ipsorum"—A very important feature—which seems to have been overlooked by some authors such as Vermeersch, Prummer, Blat, Augustine—to notice in this canon is that the words, "ipsorum ecclesiae" and "ipsorum coemeterium" are prominently employed.[115] It is apparent, according to the rules of grammar, that "ipsorum" refers to "religiosi et clerici saeculares," not to "quos." The consequence of this is that the prohibition affects only the inducing to sepulture in their

---

110 C. 1, III, 12, in Vito; Reiffenstuel, l. c., Tit. XXVIII, No. 33; Many, l. c., No. 165.

111 Constitution of Pius IX, 12 Oct., 1869=Coll. P. F. No. 1348.

112 C. 3, V, 8, in Clem.; Many, l. c., 165, d.; D'Angelo, l. c., page 58.

113 Can. 19.

114 Ferraris, "Sepult." l. c., No. 120; Moulart, l. c., p. 168; Many, l. c., 165; Coronata, l. c., No. 192, 6'.

115 Vermeersch, l. c., No. ; Prummer, l. c., No. 376; Blat, l. c., No. 85; Augustine, l. c., p. 131.

(religious and clerics) churches and cemeteries. If the case might happen that a pastor of parish A should induce a person to choose a church in parish B for the funeral services, then not only would this prohibition not obtain, but this election would be valid.[116]

(4) *The Church Selected*

The law allows election or choice of the following churches:

a. Parish churches—It is evident that terms refer here to parish churches other than the parochial church of the person. It matters not whether this parish church is attended by Regulars or by Secular clergy. Parish churches possess this right exclusively (except when a special privilege obtained) until the thirteenth century when Gregory IX allowed the churches of regulars to be suitable for election.

b. Churches of Regulars—They enjoy equal rights with parish churches in regards to this detail of the election; both are regulated by common law. In using the term "regulares," the New Code excludes the churches belonging to Religious with simple vows.[117] Likewise are excluded the churches belonging to Sisterhoods (with an exception which will be treated later).[118] The churches of Sisters with solemn vows, "moninales," may be chosen by certain females who have lived habitually within the enclosure of the convent as servants, or for educational purposes, or as patients or guests. Consequently, all outsiders are excluded from electing a church of the "moniales."

c. Patronal churches—The patron of a church may choose this one for his funeral services. This is more of an exception, since it is limited only to these patrons exclusively.[119]

---

116 C. 1, III, 12, in Vito; C. 3, V, 8, in Clem.; Ferraris, l. c., "Sepult.," No. 118, Many, l. c., No. 165, 6', b.; Coronata, l. c., No. 192, 6'.

117 Can. 488.

118 Can. 1225.

119 Wernz, l. c., Tom. II, No. 430; Ojetti, l. c., "Jus Patronatus," No. 2577.

d. Privileges—Besides the churches listed above, other churches may, by virtue of particular law, or by a concession from the Holy See or from the Bishop, obtain this right—"jus funerandi." Public and semi-private oratories are allowed all ecclesiastical functions unless excepted by the Ordinary, or excluded by the Rubrics.[120] Of course, it must be remembered that special legislation in particular cases, may cause restrictions—such as that for the church or oratories of "moniales."[121]

e. Cemetery selected—If the cemetery selected be in one place and the church selected for the funeral, in another—even though this cemetery be strictly parochial, this fact would not interfere with the right of the selected church.[122] If no church had been selected, then the church of the funeral would be that one which is attached to the parochial cemetery, or that one to which the cemetery of the Religious belongs; otherwise, the proper church would be the cathedral church, and lacking this—the church of the parish in which the cemetery is located.[123]

(5) *Fact of Election*

a. Making the election—One may choose the church of the funeral himself or through another lawfully commissioned for this purpose.[124] If the election is made through another, he can fulfill the mandate even after the death of the person who gave the mandate.[125] Any person at all may be eligible to act as the agent.[126]

b. Proving the election—(a) The election or the mandate, is never presumed but must be proved.[127] The fact of this election or the granting of the mandate may be proved in various ways.

---

120 Cans. 1191, 1193.
121 Can. 1225.
122 Coronata, l. c., No. 188, No. 103.
123 Can. 1230, No. 7.
124 Can. 1226, No. 1.
125 Can. 1226, No. 2.
126 Coronata, l. c., No. 194.
127 A. A. Sedis, Vol. XIII, page 534, 9 Jul., 1921.

(1) Testimony of two witnesses.[128] If these witnesses should disagree, not in regards to the fact of election, but in regards to the designated church, then by conjecture and reasoning may be determined which of these two churches, the person most probably had elected.[129]

(2) Statement in the will, testament or codicil even though it be invalid.[130]

(3) A private document signed by the person.[131]

(4) Testimony of the person's confessor, or pastor, providing that this testimony does not favor his own advantage.[132]

(5) The acquiescent signs, or nods of the person, if he is unable to speak, is sufficient to demonstrate his wish and choice.[133]

(b) The above rules can be applied to the proving of the mandate if such were given.

(c) Except the one commissioned with the mandate, no other can elect the sepulture of the deceased.[134]

(d) Note that this election must be definite and certain. It would not be sufficient to prove a mere desire or wish of the person.[135]

4. The Church of the Funeral for Those Possessing "Sepulchra Majorum"

(1) *Canonical Rights*

Notwithstanding the preeminence with which the New Code adorns parochial rights in regards to the funeral church, certain rights and privileges are still allowed those who have title to ancestral burying places and the like. The question arises as to which would be

128 S. C. C., 13 Feb., 1666.

129 S. C. C., 19 Dec., 1739; Coronata, l. c., No. 195.

130 S. C. C., 13 Feb., 1666; Moulart, l. c., p. 162; Many, l. c., No. 165.

131 Coronata, l. c., No. 195.

132 Schmalzgrueber, l. c., Tit. '888, No. 26, Moulart, l. c., p. 165; Many, l. c., No. 165.

133 D'Angelo, l. c., p. 59.

134 Can. 1226; Coronata, l. c., No. 195.

135 Coronata, l. c., No. 195.

the church of the funeral in the case of one, having parochial attachment, not having chosen any special church—but possessing title to "sepulchra majorum." Would the proper church of the funeral be that one of the place in which this "sepulchrum majorum" is located? According to the old law, the church of "sepulchra majorum" enjoyed rights of preeminence over all excepting a church of election.[136] "Where no wish has been expressed it will be presumed that the interment is to take place in any vault or burial place which may have belonged to the deceased or his family."[137] The New Code rather stresses the importance due the rights of the parish. Nevertheless, the Code admits of this rights of "sepulchra majorum." Although this canon does not mention expressly the discipline regarding the church of the funeral, however it treats of sepulture in general.[138] For, the principle—"ubi fumulus ibi funus"—and the title of this chapter in the Code—"the transferring of the body to the church, the funeral and burial"—at once suggests that the church of the funeral may be that one pertaining to the "sepulchra majorum." Thus, if one died without having expressed any wish for the funeral to take place at any specified church, the body could be legitimately transferred to the church pertaining to the cemetery in which is located his ancestral plot or tomb. This resolution is supported by Canon 1230 #7—"If a body is sent to a place where the deceased did not have a parish of his own, the right to conduct all the funeral services pertains to the cathedral church, or lacking this, to the pastor of the church where the cemetery in which the body is to be buried, is located."

---

136 C. 1, 3, XIII, 28; C. 3, III, 12, in Vito; Schmalzgrueber, l. c., Tit. XXVIII; Ferraris, l. c., No. 15, sq.; Moulart, l. c., p. 172, sq.; Devoti, l. c., p. 546; Many, l. c., No. 167, sq.; Wernz, l. c., No. 785; D'Angelo, l. c., p. 51, sq.

137 Cath. Encyc. "Burial."

138 Can. 1229, No. 1.

(2) *Special Regulations*

a. For the church of the funeral to be that one pertaining to the "sepulchra majorum," it is taken for granted that no other special church had been elected.[139]

b. If this church was quite distant from the place of death, so that the body could not be conveniently transported there, and if the relatives or friends would not assume the expenses of this transportation, then the church of the funeral would be that one determined by common law[140]

c. If the husband has title to a "sepulchrum majorum," the wife is entitled to burial there, and it follows, that the church of the funeral will be that one of the burial place. If the wife had married several times, the church of the funeral will be that one of her last husband.[141]

d. If the deceased had title to several "sepulchra majorum," the family or heirs are to choose the place of burial, and likewise the church of the funeral will be that one of the place selected.[142]

e. It must be borne in mind that all the above remarks suppose that the deceased had not elected any special church.

f. Since the rules governing the proper funeral church in these cases are practically identical with the rules governing the "sepulchra majorum" themselves, refer to Section I, page 37, of this treatise for a more detailed discussion.

---

139 Can. 1229, No. 1; Coronata, l. c., No. 202.
140 Can. 1218, No. 3.
141 Can. 1229, No. 2.
142 Can. 1229, No. 3.

PART III. THE MINISTER OF THE FUNERAL SERVICES

CHAPTER I. THE MINISTER FROM COMMON LAW

The common and ordinary law of the church regarding the funeral services, prescribes that the church of the funeral should be the parish church, and the pastor, the proper minister. Special law and various rights or privileges, except from the binding force of this law. Consequently, in discussing the regulations of the common law, it is to be taken for granted that exemptions or exceptions are not in effect.

1. When Death Occurred in One's Own Parish

The proper church of the funeral is one's parish church, and the proper minister is the pastor. If one belongs to several parishes, the pastor of one's parish in which death occurred, is the proper minister.[1] Likewise, the prescription that, "in doubt, the rights of one's parish always prevail"—applies also to the minister.[2] The pastor has not only the right but also the duty to go to the house, or send another priest—to perform the required ceremonies there, then to conduct the body to the church for the funeral services.[3] This obligation is grave since only a grave cause will excuse. From the entire service, the excusing cause would have to be very serious—such as in time of war, pestilence, illness of the priest.[4] But to excuse from that part of the services which consists in the conducting of the body to the church, the reason would not have to be so grave. This custom does not obtain in some countries, as in

1 Can. 1216, No. 2.
2 Can. 1217.
3 Can. 1230, No. 1; Wernz, l. c., No. 776.
4 Ferraris, l. c., "Sepult.," No. 150; Coronata, l. c., No. 206.

America for instance where distance renders it impossible, and the paucity or priests and lack of time would permit the omission of this part of the service.[5] The custom of holding the services at the house and then proceeding directly to the cemetery, is reprobated, and considered an abuse which should be prudently abolished.[6]

(2) *When Death Occurred Outside One's Own Parish*

As we have already discussed—the church of the funeral in this case, would be the parish church of the deceased, and of course, the minister of the services would be the pastor. But when one died in a strange parish, who is the lawful minister who shall conduct the body to the parish church of the deceased as prescribed by law?

a. The New Code states, that in such a case, when the body can be conveniently brought to the person's own parish church, his parish priest has the right and duty to enter the other parish to perform the ceremonies at the house, and to conduct the body to his parish church for the services.[7] The canon prescribes that this priest must previously inform the pastor of the parish where the person died.

b. In the case where this would be very inconvenient on account of distance, etc., and the relatives were looking after the arrangements, which priest may perform the ceremony of the "levandi cadaveris," at the house? It would seem that this same principle of Canon 1230 #2, would still hold good since the New Code does not state otherwise.[8]

c. If transportation were highly inconvenient, and the relatives or friends were not willing to make the arrangements and assume the expenses, then the prescription of Canon 1218 #1, would follow, whereby

5 Coronata, l. c., No. 207; Augustine, l. c., p. 135; Murphy, l. c., p. 2.

6 S. C. R., 21 Apr., 1783, No. 3291; 28 Feb., 1920=A. A. S., Vol. XII, p. 128.

7 Canon 1230, No. 2.

8 Coronata, l. c., No. 207, 1'.

the pastor of the parish in which death occurred, would be the lawful minister.

d. If the deceased had belonged to several parishes, then the legitimate and proper minister would be the pastor of the parish proper to the deceased which is the nearer at hand.[9]

CHAPTER II. THE MINISTER FROM SPECIAL LAW

For certain persons, there are special rules and privileges governing the church of their funeral services—likewise there are special rules and privileges governing the proper minister of the service.

(1) *Roman Pontiff*

The proper ministers of the funeral services of the Roman Pontiff are the Cardinals.[1] If death occurred away from Rome, or if the Holy Father had selected a special church, yet in all cases, the Cardinals must conduct the services. In the Constitution of Pius X "Vacante Sede," are designated and described minutely the various ceremonies and formalities.[2]

(2) *Cardinals*

Ordinarily the Roman Pontiff designates the various items of the funeral proceedings, when death has occurred in Rome. Otherwise, the Dean of the Sacred College is the proper minister of the funeral of Cardinals dying in Rome.[3] If death occurred outside of Rome, the dignitaries and canons of the cathedral of this place have not only the right but also the duty of conducting the services.[4] If the cathedral was not

9 Can. 1218, No. 2.

1 Motu Proprio, Pius XI, March, 1922=A. A. S. Vol. XIV, p. 145.
2 25 Dec., 1904=Appendix to the New Code.
3 Wernz, l. c., No. 775; D'Angelo, l. c., p. 48.
4 Can. 1230, No. 6; 399, No. 3; Coronata, l. c., No. 209, 2'.

located in the place of death, then the rector of the more prominent church would be the proper minister, unless the Cardinal had selected another church.[5]

(3) *Bishops*

The dignitaries and canons are the proper ministers of the funeral.[6] If death occurred outside the episcopal city, and transportation to the city cannot be arranged, then the rector of the more prominent church of this vicinity is to take charge of the proceedings. In the case of titular Bishops, where no church has been selected and no title to "sepulchra majorum," then the right and duty of the minister falls upon the pastor of the deceased, according to common law.[7]

(4) *Priests*

The proper minister for the funeral of priests and beneficiaries is he who has charge of the church which is the proper one for the funeral, determined by common or special law, or by election or title to ancestral sepulture. (See Part II, page 64.) Since the general law does not make any special designation of the minister for the funeral services of priests, sometimes, particular law reserves this office to the urban or rural dean.[8]

(5) *Religious*

a. The pastor of a Religious is his Superior, consequently he is the proper minister for the funeral.

b. If death occurred outside the Religious House, it is befitting that the pastor of this place be notified of the transporting of the body.[9]

c. If death occurred outside the Religious House, and transportation is highly inconvenient, and no one

---

5 Ferraris, l. c., "Sepult.," No. 60; Moulart, l. c., p. 195; Ojetti, l. c., "Exequiae," No. 2155; Coronata, l. c., No. 209, 3'.

6 Can. 1230, No. 6; 397, No. 3; Wernz, l. c., No. 775; Coronata, l. c., No. 210.

7 Many, l. c., No. 175.

8 Wernz, l. c., No. 775.

9 Cans. 1221, Nos. 1, 2; 1230, No. 2.

will offer to assume the expenses for such, then the proper minister would be the pastor of the place.

d. If the servants of Religious have rights to funeral services in the Religious House, then the Superior would be the proper minister. If another church had been selected, the pastor of this church would be the lawful minister.[10] If death occurred within the enclosure, the Superior performs the first ceremonies over the corpse ("levare corpus").[11] If the death occurred outside the enclosure, the pastor of this place has the right to the performance of this ceremony.[12]

(6) *Guests, Students and Patients of Religious*

If such persons have the privilege of having their funeral services in the church exempt from the jurisdiction of the pastor, as we have already discussed—then the proper minister would be the Superior of this church. If the corpse is to be transported to this Religious church, the right is still reserved to the local pastor (of the parish in which this house, college or hospital is located) to the first ceremonies over the body, and the conducting of the corpse to the funeral church.[13]

(7) *Seminarians*

For those who die in a Seminary the Rector of the Seminary is the proper minister of the funeral services. If another church had been elected, the Rector has still the right to perform the first ceremonies—"levare corpus."[14]

(8) *Sisters*

a. Those exempt from parochial jurisdiction—(a) If death occurred in this house, the minister of the entire funeral service is the Chaplain of the community.[15]

---

10 Can. 1230, No. 3.
11 Can. 1221, Nos. 1, 3.
12 Can. 1221, No. 3; 1230, No. 3.
13 Cans. 1222; 1230, No. 3; Coronata, l. c., No. 212, 7'-8'.
14 Cans. 1222; 1230, No. 3; 1368.
15 Can. 1230, No. 5.

Note that this right is restricted to the Chaplain, to the exclusion of the confessor. This applies to all Sisters, whether "moniales" or "sorores," providing they are exempt from parochial jurisdiction.[16] Novices are entitled to this privilege providing they have not selected another church.

(b) If death occurred outside their house—The New Code states that the general law of the canons is to be observed.[17] Thus, the minister of the funeral ceremonies will be the pastor of the parish where death occurred, when transportation to the Religious House is inconvenient, and no one will defray the expenses.[18] But if the body is brought to the house, then the funeral services are to be conducted by the Chaplain.[19]

b. Those not exempt from parochial jurisdiction—These Sisters are considered as having a domicile in the parish in which their house is located. Consequently, the proper minister for their funeral services will be the parish priest.[20]

CHAPTER III. THE MINISTER FOR THOSE WHO HAD ELECTED THE CHURCH

As a general rule, the rector of the elected church, will be the proper minister for the funeral services. Exceptions from this rule may follow from various modes of election, and the species of church elected.

(1) *Cemetery Alone Selected*

When the cemetery alone has been selected—no special church having been chosen, the right to the funeral services pertains to the cathedral church of this place. Where there is no cathedral, the funeral services

16 Can. 464, No. 2.
17 Can. 1230, No. 5.
18 Cans. 1218, Nos. 1, 2, 3; 1221, No. 2.
19 Can. 1221, Nos. 1, 2.
20 Can. 1230, Nos. 1, 2, 5; Maroto, l. c., Tom. I, No. 410, not. 2.

would be conducted by the pastor of the parish in which the cemetery is located. The New Code wisely adds that local custom or diocesan statutes may regulate otherwise.[1]

(2) *Church Alone Selected*

If the church alone has been elected, no special cemetery being chosen—the rector of this church will be the proper minister.

a. If the church elected is an exempt one, the parish priest of the deceased may perform the first ceremonies and conduct the corpse to the church—then the rector of this exempt church takes charge of the following services.[2] This dividing of the ceremonies might in some cases, be highly inconvenient on account of distance, lack of time and so on—then it seems probable that the rector of the exempt church could take charge of the entire service.[3] A particular custom may obtain in some places against this common law.[4]

b. If the church elected is not exempt from parochial jurisdiction the funeral services are to be performed by the pastor of the parish in which this church is located—providing that the deceased was a parishioner of the pastor.[5] It is evident that this regulation is limited in extent, and it is clear from the canon, that if the deceased were not a parishioner of the parish in which the elected church is located, whether exempt or not, then his own pastor has the right to perform those initial ceremonies, while the rector of the elected church conducts the remaining services.[6]

c. If a church belonging to Sisters, was elected by those who are allowed this privilege, the parish priest of the deceased, or the pastor of the place where death occurred, has the right to the initial ceremonies. If

1 Can. 1230, No. 7.
2 Can. 1230, No. 3.
3 Many, l. c., No. 195; Coronata, l. c., No. 217.
4 S. C. C., 14 Sep., 1878.
5 Can. 1230, No. 4.
6 Can. 1230, No. 2; Coronata, l. c., No. 217, b.

death had occurred inside the Religious House, the chaplain is the proper minister for the entire function.[7]

d. If a church had been elected by reason of right of patronage, the right to the initial ceremonies still belongs to the pastor of the deceased.[8]

CHAPTER IV. THE MINISTER FOR THOSE HAVING TITLE TO "SEPULCHRA MAJORUM"

This right to special burial plots is equivalent to election of sepulture. Consequently the same rules which concern the proper minister of the funeral ceremonies of elective sepulture, will apply here also.[1] In general the pastor of the deceased retains the right to the initial ceremonies (levare corpus) notwithstanding where the interment is to take place.

CHAPTER V. SPECIAL DUTIES OF THE MINISTER

1. The Mourners

The pastor cannot, except for a just and serious cause—approved by the Ordinary, prevent secular, Religious, and pious societies, who have been invited by the family or heirs of the deceased—from coming to assist at the funeral services and at the service in the church.[1] Preference is to be tendered the clergy attached to the church of the funeral services, by the members of

7 Cans. 1225, 1230, Nos. 3, 4.
8 Cans. 1225, 1230, Nos. 3, 4; 1232, No. 2.

1 Can. 1230, Nos. 3, 4.

1 Can. 1233, No. 1.

the family in the matter of invitation to the services.[2] This prescription of the New Code appears at first glance, rather superfluous. But the value and importance of the injunction is evident when disputes arise over delicate situations regarding the funeral arrangements.[3] The mourners and all who assist at the funeral must respect the orders of the pastor in the arrangement of the funeral procession with due regard to the rights of precedence which certain personages enjoy.[4] The pastor may decide in which direction or through which streets the procession should proceed.[5] Clerics must never act as pall-bearers for a defunct layman, no matter what his rank or dignity may have been.[6]

2. Insignia

The New Code states that Societies and their insignia which are manifestly inimical to the Catholic Religion, are never to be admitted to the funeral services. In regards to the Societies—the consequences are evident. In regards to the various insignia, emblems, banners and the like, of societies and associations—certain features are to be noted.

(1) If they are manifestly impious and irreligious, they are to be refused countenance.[7] Note this requirement that they be "manifestly" impious; this fact should be well ascertained. If such are brought into the church, they must be removed before any of the ceremonies may commence; if they are not removed, the clergy should withdraw unless Mass has already begun. Then a solemn protest should be lodged by the ecclesiastical authorities.[8]

---

2 Can. 1233, No. 1.
3 Coronata, l. c., No. 221.
4 Can. 1233, No. 3; 106; 491.
5 S. C. R., 19 Dec., 1671, ad. 5, No. 1440.
6 Can. 1233, No. 4.
7 Wernz, l. c., No. 783.
8 S. C. S. Off., 2 Dec., 1840; 1 Aug., 1855; 2 Jul., 1878; S. C. S. Off., 3 Oct., 1887; 24 Nov., 1899; S. C. R., 14 Jul., 1887.

(2) The emblems, banners and the like, of Catholic societies and confraternities, which have been blessed, may be admitted.[9] They must, however have some Religious significance in their composition.

(3) National emblems, flags, colors, etc., may be tolerated in certain circumstances, providing there is not the slightest contempt shown the Church or the Sacred Liturgy.[10]

3. "Liber Defunctorum"

After the funeral, the minister shall enter in the "liber defunctorum"—"book of the dead"—the name and age of the deceased; the name of the parents or spouse; the date of death; who administered the Sacraments; what Sacraments were given; and, the place and date of the funeral.[11] There is a serious obligation on the part of the pastor to have this record, and keep it properly.[12] The formula for entering this record is outlined by the Roman Ritual, as follows:

"Anno . . . . die . . . . mensis . . . . N, filius vel filia N., ex loco N., aetatis N., in domo N., in communione S. Matris Ecclesiae animarum Deo reddidit; cujus corpus die . . . . sepultum est in Ecclesia S. N.; mihi N., vel N., confessario probato, confessus die . . . . , Sanctissimoque Viatico refectus die . . . . et Sacri Olei unctione roboratus per me, die, ... etc."[13]

PART IV. BURIAL SERVICES

In treating of the ecclesiastical law regarding burial services, it is not necessary to go into much detail, since this has been discussed—for the most part—in the preceding PARTS. Only the particular regulations

---

9 S. C. S. Off., 3 Sep., 1882; S. C. R., 11 Jul., 1887; Bargilliat, l. c., No. 1420.

10 S. Poen., 4 Apr., 1887; 22 March, 1911; Bargilliat, l. c., No. 1420.

11 Can. 1238.

12 Can. 470.

13 Tit. X, Cap. 7.

which deal with the interment will be treated in this PART.

CHAPTER I. THE PLACE OF BURIAL

1. Common Law

The general rule to follow is that, the funeral services having been completed, the body is to be interred in the cemetery attached to this church.[1] This cemetery may be a strictly parochial one, or one used in common by several parishes.

2. Special Law

It is clear that the exceptions by reason of special law, whereby certain personages are entitled to special burying places, retain their full vigor. The various details of this law have been treated and discussed at length already, and require no examination in this PART.

3. Elective Burial Places

A broad measure of freedom has always been extended by ecclesiastical law in the matter of electing the cemetery for one's interment. The New Code continues this policy and states definitely the various regulations concerning this election. However, not in the Chapter I treating of cemeteries, does the Code place these particular regulations, but in the Chapter II in treating of the funeral services. In commenting on this latter chapter in Parts II and III the rules and various items of procedure have been explained at some length. And since the laws of the election of cemeteries and that of the funeral church, are for the most part identical—

1 Can. 1231, No. 1; Schmalzgrueber, l. c., Tit. XXVIII, No. 1.

it will be sufficient here to remark only the particular regulations which deal more or less exclusively with the election of cemeteries.

(1) *Those Who May Choose*

All excepting children who have not attained the age of puberty, and professed Religious—may select their cemetery.[2]

(2) *The Cemetery of Election*

a. Any cemetery whatsoever may be selected independently of the church of the funeral, unless, of course, the authorities of the cemetery refuse admission.[3]

b. Even cemeteries belonging exclusively to Religious, may be legitimately elected.[4] The permission of the Superior must be obtained; and this may be granted insofar as the Constitutions of the respective Communities allow him. If the constitutions contain nothing to the contrary, or no enactment at all on this subject, the local Superior is certainly competent.[5]

c. Note that the New Code mentions only the election of cemeteries to the exclusion of ancestral tombs, "sepulchra majorum." The latter, of course, are not cemeteries, properly so-called.

(3) *Liberty of Election*

Religious and the secular clergy are strictly forbidden to induce anyone to vow, swear, give word of honor, or in any way to promise that he will choose their (Religious or Seculars) cemeteries for burial; if this occurs, the election will be null and void.[6] This canon has been treated in detail on page .

(4) *Making and Proving Election*

Anyone may choose the cemetery whether by himself or through another by mandate. If the election is to be

2 Cans. 1223, 1224.
3 Can. 1228.
4 Schmalzgrueber, l. c., Tit. XXVIII, No. 17.
5 Coronata, l. c., No. 193; Augustine, l. c., p. 132.
6 Can. 1227.

made by another, he may apply this mandate even after the death of the person. The fact of this election or the concession of the mandate, may be proved in any legal form.[7]

4. "Sepulchra Majorum"

Provided that the necessary permission has been obtained, one may have a private burial place.[8] Generally, these locations are understood as ancestral burial places—"sepulchra majorum."[9]

(1) *Species*

a. Family plots—in which only the members of the family of the deceased, may be buried.

b. Hereditary plots or tombs—in which none other besides the person and his heir may be buried, whether of the family or not; and this to the exclusion of the members of his family who are not his heirs.

c. Mixed plots or tombs—(both family and hereditary)—in which both the family and the heirs may be buried.

d. Other private plots and tombs—The old law recognized the three species listed above while the New Code adds another type, namely—those locations selected by and reserved to the use of a determined group, society or confraternity, e. g.—such as a non-exempt congregation with simple vows.[10]

(2) *Erection of "sepulchra majorum"*

a. Who are allowed—Any of the faithful may erect for themselves and their relatives, special burying places.[11] It is evident that individual Religious are not included. Associations and private families may be entitled to this.[12]

---

7 Can. 1226.

8 Cans. 1208, 1209.

9 Ferraris, l. c., "Sepult.," No. 153; Moulart, l. c., p. 177, sq.; Many, l. c., No. 166; Coronata, l. c., No. 196, sq.

10 Coronata, l. c., No. 197.

11 Can. 1209, No. 1.

12 Can. 1208, No. 3.

b. Conditions required—(a) The definite designation of the place must be made.[13]

(b) Permission of the proper ecclesiastical authority. If the location is in a parochial cemetery, permission of the Ordinary of the place or his delegate, must be obtained.[14] If in a cemetery belonging to Religious, the permission of the Superior must be obtained.

(c) This permission must be had in writing.[15] The document should denote the determined type of grave desired, i. e.—whether a family, hereditary, or mixed, or otherwise.[16]

(3) *Those Entitled to Burial in "Sepulchra Majorum"*

a. All who have obtained the required permission to erect a special sepulture, thereby obtain the right to interment therein.

b. The members of the family have right to interment in the family plot. Heirs who are not members of the family, have no right to this special family plot.

c. The heirs have right to burial in hereditary plots. Members of the family who are not the heirs, have not this right.

d. Members of a congregation, society, etc., which possesses a special plot have title to burial therein.

e. The members of the family and also the heirs have title to burial in the so-called mixed plots.

f. The wife is entitled to the burial place of her husband, and if she had been married repeatedly, that of her last husband.[17] It is clear from this canon, that a special place—the right to which belongs to the wife alone—cannot be urged against the right to the plot or tomb of her husband. Some authors have maintained in the past, that likewise, the husband is entitled to the

13 Coronata, l. c., No. 198.
14 Can. 1209, No. 1.
15 Can. 1209, No. 1.
16 Coronata, l. c., No. 198.
17 Can. 1229, No. 2; C. 2, C. 13, q. 2; C. 3, III, 12, in Vito; Schmalzgrueber, l. c., Tit. XXVIII, No. 31.

burial place of his wife.[18] Others deny that the term "husband" and "wife" can thus be used correlatively, and that this title is restricted to the wife.[19] The latter opinion appears more tenable.[20]

g. Children and infants are entitled to burial in their family or hereditary plots. Although the New Code prescribes the setting apart of a special place for the interment of infants, yet this is not to be urged to the detriment of their right to burial in their "sepulchra majorum."[21] Such may be deduced from the words—"quatenus commode fieri potest." Both these details are repeating the old law when this practise was certainly recognized.[22]

h. It must be noted, that in regards to family or hereditary burial places, the descendants and not the ancestors have title. For example, the father would have no title to the "sepulchrum majorum," strictly proper to his son.

i. If the deceased had title to several "sepulchra majorum," his family or heirs may select which one to choose. Formerly, there was some difference of opinion concerning which types of these special plots, took precedence, and which persons were eligible for the choice between them.[23] The New Code, however, treats all equally.[24]

---

18 Reiffenstuel, l. c., Tit. XXVIII, No. 23; Ferraris, l. c., "Sepult.," No. 82.

19 Schmalzgrueber, l. c., Tit. XXVIII, Nos. 34, 35; Many, l. c., No. 169.

20 Coronata, l. c., No. 203.

21 Can. 1209, No. 3.

22 Rom. Rit. Tit. VI, Cap. 6; S. C. C., 21 Oct., 1613; 13 Mar., 1770; Ferraris, l. c., "Sepult.," No. 15; Many, l. c., No. 167, 5'; Coronata, l. c., No. 202, b.

23 Many, l. c., No. 167.

24 Can. 1229, No. 3; Vermeersch, l. c., No. 555; Coronata, l. c., 202, b.

CHAPTER II. THE MINISTER OF THE BURIAL SERVICE

The right is granted to, and the obligation imposed upon, the priest who has performed the funeral services in the church—of committing the body to burial. This priest may arrange for another priest to officiate. Only a grave necessity will excuse from this regulation.[1] In some places, there are long-standing traditions against accompanying the body to the cemetery. Especially in large cities of America, where the cemeteries are quite distant, it would seem that serious inconvenience would be caused the priest who could hardly spare the time necessary for each and every funeral procession.[2] This is permitted in the New Code.[3]

If the priest accompanies the funeral procession, he has every right to wear the stole and carry the cross in passing through another parish, or even through another diocese, without any permission of either pastor or Ordinary.[4] A decree of the S. Congregation of Rites, which counsels prudence and clerical etiquette, states that the shortest route should be followed to avoid any semblance of show, or danger of provoking others.[5]

PART V. FUNERAL FEES

The funeral fees may be defined, as—the contributions which the faithful give to the ministers on the occasion of a funeral to defray the expenses incurred and to contribute towards their support. Consequently, there can be no suspicion that these fees are considered

1 Can. 1231, No. 2.
2 American Ecclesiastical Review, July, 1922.
3 Cans. 1231, No. 2; 1232, No. 2.
4 Can. 1231, No. 1.
5 23 April, 1895, No. 3854.

as the price for the funeral services, since they are allowed for the causes mentioned.[1] The Church has ever been scrupulously careful that no hint of simony or extortion enter into these relations. The Roman Pontiffs have always condemned any abuses of this statute, and strictly forbade any refusal of the funeral services, when the fees were not forthcoming; a censure of excommunication was incurred by offenses of this nature.[2] It is hardly necessary to go into the historical or ethical phase of this detail—the traditions and authorities are clearly evident.[3] It must be remembered, that likewise, the faithful have the obligation of paying the fees determined by the diocesan statutes or customs—of course, only insofar as they are able to do so.[4]

CHAPTER I. THE SCHEDULE OF FUNERAL FEES

The New Code directs the local Ordinaries—each for his own territory—to draw up a list or schedule of funeral fees, if such does not exist already. They shall consult the Cathedral Chapter, and, if deemed advisable—the rural deans and pastors of the episcopal city. In doing so, the lawful customs of the district must be taken into consideration, as well as the circumstances of persons and times. This list should be determined in a moderate manner for the rights of all concerned, both priests and people, so that all occasion of contention and

---

1 C. 9, C. 13, q. 2.

2 Coronata, l. c., 242.

3 C. 0, 12, 14, 15; C. 13, q. 2; C. 1, 2, 3, 4, 8, 9, XIII, 28; C. 42, XV, 3; C. 2, III, 7, in Clem.; C. 2, III, 6, in Extrav. Commun.; S. C. C., 13 Nov., 1660; 24 May, 1710; 2 May, 1711; 26 Jan., 1726; Rit. Rom. Tit. VI, C. 1, n. 8; Schmalzgrueber, l. c., Tit. XXVIII, Nos. 80, 83, 91; Reiffenstuel, l. c., Tit. XXVIII, No. 70, sq.; Wernz, l. c., No. 786; Ferraris, l. c., "Taxa"; Gasparri, l. c., No. 541; Moulart, l. c., pp. 243, 254; Many, l. c., No. 201, sq.; D'Angelo, l. c., p. 159, sq.; Coronata, l. c., Nos. 243, 245.

4 Reiffenstuel, l. c., Tit. XXVIII, No. 70; Wernz, l. c., No. 778.

scandal is removed.[1] In such wise, the New Code succinctly states the entire discipline.

1. Obligations of the Ordinary

(1) The Ordinary is bound to consult the Cathedral Chapter. It is evident that he is not compelled to abide by their decisions or advices.[2] But if he would not fulfill the formal injunction of consulting with the chapter, he would then act invalidly.[3] Although he is not bound to consult with the rural deans and the pastors of the episcopal city, yet if such is opportune it should be done. For these officials will be of assistance in determining the correct scale suitable for the rural and urban districts.

(2) The Ordinary is bound to give due consideration to the particular customs and special circumstances, so that particular rights and exemptions may not suffer.

(3) The Ordinary is bound to draw up this schedule in such a manner so that the rights of all persons concerned will be clearly and reasonably determined.

(4) The Ordinary is bound to determine the "parochial portion" in this schedule, and the exact amount or ratio.[4]

(5) Although there is no obligation, the Ordinary may state in this schedule—the various classes of funerals.[5]

2. Binding Force of this Schedule

(1) All the priests of his diocese are bound to abide by this schedule. No one may demand more than is allowed, for funeral services, burial, or anniversary services. Religious pastors are certainly obliged to follow the schedule of the diocese.[6]

---

1 Can. 1234, No. 1.
2 Can. 105, No. 1.
3 Can. 105, No. 1; Coronata, l. c., No. 245.
4 Can. 1237, No. 3.
5 Can. 1234, No. 2.
6 Cans. 631; 1235, No. 1.

(2) Likewise, the people—when they are able—are bound by the regulations of this schedule. Of course, they are perfectly free to choose whatever class of funeral service that they may prefer.[7]

(3) The poor are not bound by this schedule. They are exempt from paying the funeral taxes. Moreover, the Code distinctly states that the poor shall by all means be given a decent funeral and burial, inclusive of the exsequies, free of all tax, according to the diocesan statutes and liturgical laws.[8] Consequently there may never be any curtailment of the services or ceremonies, on the excuse that there were no fees in evidence.[9] A diocesan schedule which would permit of the omission of the funeral Mass is distinctly out of harmony with this definite prescription of the Code. Of course, exceptions can readily be understood in the case of hospitals where so many deaths occur and where there is no one to look after the expenses and fees.[10]

CHAPTER II. THE PAROCHIAL PORTION

The parochial portion may be defined, as—that determined part of the funeral fees which is due the pastor of the deceased from the church which conducted the funeral.[1] It is obvious that this refers to the cases where the funeral was held in a church other than the parish church of the deceased.[2] Various terms have been employed in the past, such as—canonical portion, funeral quarter, fourth portion, etc., the reason of its existence is from the fact that when one deserts one's parish church to select a strange one for his funeral services, it is

7 Can. 1234, No. 2.
8 Can. 1235, No. 2.
9 Rom. Rit. Tit. VI, C. 1, n. 8.
10 S. C. R., 12 Jun., 1899, No. 4024; Coronata, l. c., No. 245.

1 Many, l. c., No. 201.
2 Wernz, l. c., No. 787.

only just and reasonable that some portion of the fees be handed over to the church which one attended in life.[3] At one time, a distinction was made between the episcopal and parochial portions, when still a part of the parochial portion was due the Bishop.[4] But custom has abolished the latter many years ago.[5]

The parochial portion—"portio paroecialis"—is of great antiquity. There was mention of it as early as the VIIIth century.[6] The ancient decretals manifest clearly the ecclesiastical law in this regard.[7] In the New Code, the law is stated in brief extent, and the rules to follow in every exigency are clearly set forth. Providing that there is no exception by reason of particular law, the parochial portion is due the pastor of the deceased, except in the case when the body cannot be conveniently transported to the proper parish.[8]

1. Necessary Conditions

(1) "Salvo jure particulari"—At the very outset, the canon recognizes the value and importance of particular legislation, allowing this every consideration—otherwise the common law has effect.

(2) "Fideles"—In using this term all classes of Catholics are denoted by the Code—clerical, religious, and law; unless, of course, they are exempted by particular law or privilege.

(3) "Non funerentur in propria paroecia"—This naturally supposes such funeral services to be legitimate—which may occur in cases of elective sepulture or ancestral title.

---

3 Schmalzgrueber, l. c., Tit. XXVIII, No. 83; Reiffenstuel, l. c., Tit. XXVIII, No. 46.

4 Schmalzgrueber, l. c., Tit. XXVIII, Nos. 91, 93; Reiffenstuel, l. c.; Moulart, p. 244.

5 Wernz, l. c., No. 787; Many, l. c., No. 201.

6 C. 1, XIII, 28; Wernz, l. c., No. 787.

7 C. 1, 10, XIII, 28; C. 2, III, 12, in Vito; C. 1, II, 1, in Extrav. Commun. Conc. Trid. Sess. XXV, de ref. C. 13.

8 Can. 1236, No. 1.

(4) If death had occurred at a distance removed from one's own parish, then the parochial portion would be due only when transportation of the corpse would have been inconvenient according to the norm of the New Code; and when no one cared to defray the expenses.[9] Consequently, the pastor of the place where death occurred, would not be obliged to remit the portion to the pastor of the deceased. Formerly this distinction was not commonly recognized.[10]

2. To Whom Due

The prescribed conditions having been fulfilled, the parochial portion is due to the parish priest of the deceased.[11] This term, "parocho proprio defuncto," pertains to the pastor by reason of the law of domicile or quasi-domicile—to the Superior, in regards to Novices and those who have died in the house—to the chaplain of a convent in regards to those Sisters who are exempt from parochial jurisdiction, and also in regards to those students, guests and patients of this house, who enjoy the privilege of exemption—to the rector of the seminary in regards to all who have died in the seminary.[12]

(1) If one had title to ancestral sepulture, and yet had selected another church for the funeral, no parochial portion is due the pastor of the parish in which this special burial place is located, for he is not the parish priest of the deceased.[13]

(2) If one had belonged to several parishes, to which the body can be conveniently transported, and the funeral is held elsewhere, then the parochial portion is to be divided among the several pastors of the deceased.[14] This procedure is to be observed when the conditions—

---

9 Can. 1218.

10 Ferraris, l. c., "Sepult.," Nos. 221, 331; Moulart, l. c., p. 245; Many, l. c., No. 202; Coronata, l. c., No. 248.

11 Schmalzgrueber, l. c., Tit. XXVIII, Nos. 84, 85.

12 Cans. 1221, Nos. 1, 2; 1230, No. 5; 1222; 1368; Coronata, l. c., No. 248.

13 Many, l. c., No. 202; Coronata, l. c., No. 148, d.

14 Can. 1236, No. 2; Reiffenstuel, l. c., Tit. XXVIII, No. 45.

namely, that transportation to all is convenient—is present. But when transportation is not convenient, then no parochial portion is due. If convenient to parish A and not to parish B the parochial portion is due in total to parish A alone.[15]

(3) If one belonged to several parishes, A, B and C—and death occurred in parish A—then according to the common law the funeral is to be held from this parish, unless another had been selected, and if another church had been selected the parochial portion would be due only to parish A in which death occurred—to the exclusion of parishes B and C, even though transportation to them would have been convenient.[16]

(4) Prior to the New Code, little difficulty was experienced in these complicated situations.[17] Because, that clause, "if transportation is convenient," did not modify the effect in any way.[18] But, as we have seen, the present law gives rise to new developments, although the just and beneficial result is clearly evident.

3. From Whom Due

The purpose of this law concerning the parochial portion is to reimburse the pastor of the deceased when the funeral is held elsewhere. Consequently, only those churches, which are not the person's parish, and which are not the churches of the funeral services according to common law, are bound by this obligation.[19] A church of election, or the church of the ancestral sepulture are liable to the obligation. In regards to Cathedral Canons or other residential beneficiaries who have title to special burying-places similar to "sepulchra majorum," it is evident that the parochial portion should be given to the

---

15 Can. 1216, No. 2; 1218, No. 1; 1236, No. 2.

16 Can. 1216; Many,, l. c., 202; Coronata, l. c., No. 248.

17 C. 2, III, 12, in Vito; Many, l. c., No. 202.

18 C. 2, III, 12, in Vito; Ferraris, l. c., "Sepult.," No. 330, sq.; Wernz, l. c., No. 787; Moulart, l. c., p. 244; Many, l. c., No. 202; D'Angelo, l. c., p. 154.

19 Schmalzgrueber, l. c., Tit. XXVIII, No. 86.

parish to which they had belonged.[20] This same rule would bind in the case of cardinals at Rome, having been given sepulture outside their parish.[21] Of course, since Bishops are subject to no parish priest, no priest may lay claim to a parochial portion in the case of their funerals. Particular laws, customs and privileges must always be kept in mind when dealing with this question, as in many places, exceptions are allowed by law.[22] Many Religious Orders are exempt from this regulation from a privilege granted by the Council of Trent, which still obtains.[23] In the case of death having occurred outside of one's parish, whether or not transportation to this parish would have been convenient—changes the whole aspect, as we have noted already.

4. Deduction of the Parochial Portion

The general rule is that the parochial portion should be drawn from all and only the fees which are tabulated in the diocesan schedule for the funeral and burial.[24] Consequently, there is no requirement of deduction from the fees of anniversary services, of a week, month, year, etc. No free offering which the family may make to the priest who has performed the services, is to be taxed for this portion.[25] If, for any reason, on the day of the burial, there are only held the minor functions—and the first solemn service is held one month from this day, the parochial portion shall be taken from the fees of this service.[26] Thus, with the postponement of this "first solemn service," for a month, the obligation yet remains of deducting the parochial portion. Although the funeral Mass is not absolutely necessary for the funeral services, yet the Mass is the constitutive element of solemnity of

20 Ferraris, l. c., "Canonicus," No. 14; Many, l. c., No. 202, 3'.
21 A. S. S., Vol. XV, p. 553; Reiffenstuel, l. c., Tit. XXVIII, No. 55.
22 Reiffenstuel, l. c., Tit. XXVIII, No. 55.
23 Sess. XXV, C. 13, de ref.; Coronata, l. c., No. 249.
24 Can. 1237, No. 1; Reiffenstuel, l. c., Tit. XXVIII, No. 49.
25 S. C. Ep. et Reg., 17 Sep., 1880=A. S. S. Vol. XIII, p. 421.
26 Can. 1237, No. 2.

the exequies.[27] And doubtlessly, the funeral Mass is denoted by this "primum solemne officium funebre."[28] This lapse of time is to be computed according to the rules of the New Code concerning time.[29] Thus, it is to be reckoned from the day of the burial. If the burial took place on January 5th, the computation of this month begins on January 6th at midnight and ends at midnight on the 6th of February.[30] Consequently, if this solemn service were held within those dates, or corresponding dates, the parochial portion must be forthcoming. If not within that canonical time, the portion cannot be demanded.[31]

5. Amount of the Portion

The amount or quantity of the parochial portion should be determined in the diocesan schedule of fees.[32] The Bishop, in fixing this schedule may determine the amount of this portion in one of two ways—by fixing the amount of the funeral fees and stating the exact percentage too allotted for the portion—or by defining specifically and numerically the amount of the portion for the various classes of funeral services.[33] Generally, this portion is one quarter of the funeral fees, but the bishop is perfectly free to fix any other percentage.[34] In fixing the amount, the Bishop must give due consideration to the customs of the places.[35] If the parochial church and the funeral church are of different dioceses, the amount of the parochial portion is to be determined by the schedule governing the church where the funeral is held.[36]

---

27 Rit. Rom. Tit. VI, C. 3, n. 6; S. C. R., 13 May, 1879, No. 3494; Coronata, l. c., No. 250.

28 Coronata, l. c., No. 250; Vermeersch, l. c., No. 544.

29 Cans. 31, 35.

30 Maroto, l. c., p. 257.

31 Pont. Comm. Nov. 24, 1920=A. A. S., Vol. XII, p. 576; Vermeersch, l. c., No. 544.

32 Can. 1237, No. 3.

33 Coronata, l. c., No. 251.

34 Reiffenstuel, Tit. XXVIII, No. 48; Vermeersch, l. c., No. 544; Blat, l. c., No. 97.

35 Many, l. c., No. 205.

36 Can. 1237, No. 3.

SECTION III. CONCESSION AND DENIAL OF ECCLESIASTICAL SEPULTURE

It must be remembered just what significance ecclesiastical sepulture obtains from the canonical standpoint. Ecclesiastical sepulture consists comprehensively in the bringing of the body to the church—holding the funeral services in the church—and entombing the corpse in the place legitimately appointed for the burial of the faithful departed.[1]

PART I. THOSE ALLOWED ECCLESIASTICAL SEPULTURE

All baptised persons must be given ecclesiastical sepulture, unless they are expressly denied such by the law of the church.[2] This canon is a summing up of the prescription of the Roman Ritual where it is stated that ecclesiastical sepulture must be given to all who are not expressly forbidden by ecclesiastical law.[3] Not only is there a right conceded but also an obligation is imposed by the law of the church.[4] It is manifest that this right to ecclesiastical sepulture pertains only to Catholics. Heretics, even though they have been validly baptized in their own sect, have no claim to the services of the church.

The New Code advances a step in stating decisively, that catechumens, or those preparing to embrace the Catholic Faith, may be given ecclesiastical sepulture if they had died without baptism, through no fault of their own.[5] The tenour and the general practise as followed in the former law, conforms with this. One author, how-

1 Can. 1204.
2 Can. 1239, No. 3.
3 Tit. II, C. 1, n. 16; Tit. VI, C. 1, n. 18; C. 2, n. 1; C. 6, n. 1.
4 Reiffenstuel, l. c., Tit. XXVIII, No. 76.
5 Can. 1239, No. 2.

ever, in resurrecting an ancient dispute of the Fathers in regard to the status of catechumens, maintains that they should not be granted ecclesiastical sepulture.[6] Notwithstanding his contention and his citations of various theologians—the vast majority of authors and commentators agree unanimously in extending to catechumens who had died without baptism, the right to ecclesiastical sepulture.[7] It is hardly necessary to discuss this minor dispute—the arguments for the affirmative are conclusive, and to settle the matter entirely, the New Code has reaffirmed this position by devoting a section of the canon to it.

PART II. THOSE DENIED ECCLESIASTICAL SEPULTURE

CHAPTER I. THE UNBAPTIZED

Since the unbaptized are not members of the church, they must not be admitted to ecclesiastical sepulture.[1] Included among these persons are the infants of Catholic parents dying before having been baptized.[2] It is evident that there is an exception for such infants who die with the mother before having been born.[3] Note also the explicit exception for catechumens.[4] If there is doubt of the conferring of the baptism, or doubt of the validity—such doubt would not be sufficient to exclude these persons from ecclesiastical sepulture. They cannot be declared as unbaptized when there is only a doubt.[5]

---

6 Ferraris, l. c., "Sepult.," No. 172.

7 Schmalzgrueber, l. c., Tit. XL, No. 72; Reiffenstuel, l. c., Tit. XXVIII, No. 77; Moulart, l. c., p. 126; Many, l. c., No. 217; Wernz, l. c., No. 781; Ojetti, l. c., "Sepult.," No. 3702; D'Angelo, l. c., p. 4, et al.

---

1 Can. 1239, No. 1.

2 Wernz, l. c., No. 781, not. 47.

3 II Council of Baltimore, Acta et Decreta, No. 390; Schmalzgrueber, l. c., Tit. XXVIII, No. 71; Wernz, l. c., No. 781, not. 47; Ojetti, l. c., "Sepult.," No. 3702.

4 Can. 1239, No. 2.

5 Reiffenstuel, l. c., Tit. XXVIII, No. 77; Ferraris, l. c., "Sepult.," No. 172; Coronata, l. c., No. 256.

CHAPTER II. DELINQUENTS

In using this term—delinquent, the ecclesiastical significance alone is referred to, i. e.—those persons who have disobeyed the law of the church in the serious instances which we shall discuss.

1. Necessary Conditions

Before entering into detail regarding the various offenses or delinquencies which cause the deprivation of the right to ecclesiastical sepulture, the New Code very wisely prefaces with the prescription that "persons guilty of these offenses, are to be deprived of ecclesiastical sepulture, unless they have given some signs of repentance before death."[1] The force of this canon is perceived at once when it is rendered, as follows—"ecclesiastical sepulture is not to be denied if any sign of repentance has been shown before death." This condition must always be borne in mind when dealing with these instances. The former law has been far stricter, when, for example, one died from the effects of a duel, even though he showed signs of penitence before death, still he was refused ecclesiastical sepulture.[2] With the present law in force, all that is required to escape this deprivation, is any sign of repentance whatever it may be, such as asking for the priest, kissing the crucifix, saying the Act of Contrition, and the like.[3] This deprivation is a real penalty inflicted by the church law, and as in all penalties, the milder interpretation is to be applied when possible. There must be no extension outside of the cases expressly contained in the law, with no recurring to the former law for any extension.[4]

---

1 Can. 1240, No. 1.
2 C. 1, XV, 13; Conc. Trid. Sess. XXV, de Ref., C. 19.
3 Coronata, l. c., No. 257.
4 Can. 6, 5'.

2. Delinquencies

(1) *Apostasy*

Ecclesiastical sepulture is forbidden to notorious apostates from the Christian Faith, and those who notoriously belonged to an heretical or a schismatical sect, or to Masonic societies or to other societies of that ilk.[5] Close attention must be given this requirement of "notoriety," as this has a very important bearing on the effect of the law. A delinquency is notorious when, from the evidence of the affair, it is certain so that no subterfuge can conceal it.[6] Notoriety may be of law—when, after a valid juridicial sentence which has become final and from which there is no appeal.[7] Notoriety may be of law, also—after a confession made in court, in the presence of a judge with all the formalities required to give it juridical value.[8] Notoriety may be of fact—when the delinquency is publicly known as such and that the delinquency has been committed under such circumstances that the imputability cannot be concealed by any subterfuge nor excused by any interpretation of that law.[9]

a. Apostates—By this term is meant those who have rejected Christian Revelation, not necessarily having attached themselves to any infidel cult or society.

b. Members of an Heretical Sect—The former law constituted simple heresy—without any attachment to a sect—as sufficient for incurring this penalty.[10] The New Code has mitigated this. To suffer this deprivation, attachment to an heretical sect is required.[11]

c. Members of a Schismatical Sect—Formerly, schismatics as such were not deprived of ecclesiastical

5 Can. 1240, No. 1, 1'.
6 Wernz, l. c., Tom. VI, No. 17.
7 Cans. 2197, 2'; 1902, 1904.
8 Cans. 2197, 2'; 1750.
9 Can. 2197, 3'; Sole, l. c., p. 8; Ayrinhac, l. c., p. 29.
10 C. 8, 13, 15, XV, 7; Pius IX, Const. "Apos. Sed.," 12 Oct., 1869, IV=Coll. No. 1348; Wernz, l. c., Tom. III, No. 781; Moulart, l. c., p. 272, sq.; Many, l. c., No. 219.
11 Vermeersch, l. c., No. 549; Coronata, l. c., No. 258.

sepulture by reason of their schism. In most cases, however, schismatics were thus deprived, on account of accompanying heresy, or excommunication.[12] The New Code distinctly provides that this deprivation is due all who are notoriously addicted to a schismatical sect, even though not guilty of heresy or under excommunication.

d. Members of Masonic Societies, and others of the like—When Catholics join these forbidden societies they are looked upon as public sinners. The canon admits of societies other that those expressly condemned by the Holy See, consequently, those who belong to anti-clerical, anarchical and revolutionary societies, would likewise incur this deprivation.[13] These latter societies must be of the type described in the New Code as conspiring—"Machinatio"—clandestinely secretly, or otherwise plotting against the church, the Holy Father, the rights of the church, or those extreme socialists and Nihilists who plot to destroy the civil authority by violent means. But those mild socialists who make plans against the State by means not contrary to the natural law, such as by oratorical onslaughts, political campaigns, election dodges and the like, are not classed in this group.[14] Also remember that the addiction must have been notorious.

e. Persons excommunicated or interdicted after a condemnatory or declaratory sentence.[15] Before the New Code, excommunicated persons were classed as "vitandi" or "tolerati;" while "tolerati" could be notorious public or occult. The commentators were unanimous in stating that "vitandi" were to be denied ecclesiastical sepulture. In regards to "tolerati," there was no question of doubt regarding the "tolerati occulti"—they were not to be refused ecclesiastical sepulture. But in regards to the "tolerati notorii," opinion was divided. This was caused by conflicting

---

12 Reiffenstuel, l. c., Tit. XXVIII, No. 78; D'Angelo, l. c., p. 7; Many, l. c., No. 219.

13 S. C. S. Off., 5 Jul., 1878=Coll. P. F., No. 1405; Coronata, l. c., No. 258.

14 Can. 2339; Blat, l. c., No. 101.

15 Can. 1240, No. 1, 4'.

interpretations of the Constitution of Martin V—"Ad evitanda." One opinion held, that by this constitution, even "tolerati notorii" should be allowed ecclesiastical sepulture.[16] The other opinion claimed by the same Constitution, that "tolerati notorii" should be denied it.[17]

According to the New Code, "excommunicati," are either "vitandi" or "tolerati;" and "tolerati" are divided into "tolerati simpliciter" and "tolerati post sententiam condemnatoriam vel declaratoriam."[18] Thus, by the present law the former dispute is settled. All "excommunicata vitandi" and those "tolerati post sententiam condemnatoriam vel declaratoriam" are denied ecclesiastical sepulture. If an excommunicated person, before dying, gave some signs of repentance, ecclesiastical sepulture would not be refused. Of course, before interment, the excommunication must have been absolved by the competent authority, so as to permit of this. The form for such a post mortem absolution is contained in the Ritual.[19]

Those who have been personally interdicted are also denied ecclesiastical sepulture.[20] Such censure must likewise have been inflicted by a declaratory or condemnatory sentence.

(3) *Suicide*

Ecclesiastical sepulture is denied those who have deliberately killed themselves.[21] Since this penalty is a grave one, it must be clearly established that the person really and with deliberation had taken his life. Appearances are often deceitful; and the mere fact of discovering that death was caused by drowning, suffocation,

---

16 Schmalz., l. c., Tit. XXVIII, No. 59; Devoti, l. c., p. 548; Many, l. c., No. 218.

17 Reiff., l. c., Tit. XXVIII, No. 85; Wernz, l. c., No. 781; Moulart, l. c., p. 272; D'Angelo, l. c., p. 6=S. C. S. Off., 9 Aug., 1876, Coll. P. F., No. 1462.

18 Cans. 2258, 2259.

19 Tit. III, C. 4.

20 Const. Pius IX, "Apos. Sed.," VI, 2=Coll. P. F., No. 1348; Cans. 1240, No. 1, 2'; 2275, 4'.

21 Can. 1240, No. 1, 3'; Schmalzgrueber, l. c., Tit. XXVIII, No. 64.

violence, etc., would not be sufficient to prove it suicidal.[22] Insanity of course, would excuse from this penalty, although this condition must first be proved.[23] Likewise, signs of repentance must not be presumed, but proved.[24] This "deliberato consilio," mentioned in the Canon, must be given every consideration in these serious cases. Any testimony which shows that the person was not in his right mind when committing suicide, would exempt from the penalty.[25]

(4) *Duelling*

They who have died in a duel or from a wound received in a duel, are denied ecclesiastical sepulture.[26] The old law was more severe on this point. Duelling was, at one time, a rather wide-spread evil, and the church had to take stringent measures to stamp it out.[27] Even though the duellers gave ample signs of repentance before their death, yet ecclesiastical sepulture was forbidden them.[28]

The New Code mitigates this former severity and allows of any sign of repentance causing the lifting of the penalty. Of course, by duelling, are meant only those vindictive and violent combats, whether or not the formalities of procedure had been observed.[29] In no way can this penalty be applied to sporting events, such as prize fights, or bull fights, from which death sometimes follows.

(5) *Ordering Cremation*

The deprivation of ecclesiastical sepulture is incurred by all who had ordered the cremation of their body, and who had not retracted this command before

---

22 Many, l. c., No. 220.

23 S. C. S. Off., 16 May, 1866=Coll. P. F., No. 1290; Rom. Rit. Tit. VI, C. 2, n. 3.

24 Rom. Rit. Tit. VI, C. 2, n. 3.

25 Coronata, l. c., No. 260.

26 Can. 1240, No. 1, 4'.

27 Reiffenstuel, l. c., Tit. XXVIII, No. 79, 80, 81.

28 C. 1, 2, XV, 13; Conc. Trid. Sess. XXV, Cap. 19, de ref.; Wernz, l. c., No. 781, n. III; Many, l. c., No. 220.

29 Many, l. c., No. 220.

dying.[30] It is evident that this deprivation would not follow if the cremation had been ordered by others without the person's wish or intention. It is possible that one could be in good faith and order the cremation of his body, and since this would not be imputable as he would not be morally culpable of a delinquency—the penalty would not follow.[31] The order for cremation of one's body must have been given for the penalty to be incurred. The fact that one belonged to a crematorial society, worked in a crematory, or legislated for its practice, etc., would not induce the deprivation unless one actually had commanded that his own body should be cremated.[32] Of course, any rescinding of such an order would excuse from the penalty of deprivation.

(6) *Other Public and Manifest Sinners*[33]

This final class on account of its wide extension, presents a difficulty, and must be interpreted with exactness and the law applied with great care. "Odiosa restringenda sunt"—the terms of this paragraph must be examined with due strictness to prevent any odious extension. The New Code defines a public crime as one which has already been divulged or one which occurred in such circumstances, that it can easily be adjudged and must become public.[34] "With a public crime must not be confused a manifest crime which requires that a greater number of positive witnesses who, through their certain knowledge and physical senses, thoroughly know of the affair and moreover can give testimony of it."[35] With this assertion in mind, and noting that the Code has added "manifest" along with "public," we venture the opinion that it is possible that one might have committed a public crime, yet would not be a public sinner in this canonical signification. The sinner must be known

30 S. C. S. Off., 15 Dec., 1886=Coll. P. F., No. 1665.
31 Can. 1229, No. 3, 1'; Sole, l. c., No. 117.
32 Coronata, l. c., No. 132.
33 Can. 1240, No. 1, 6'.
34 Can. 2197, 1'.
35 Wernz, l. c., Tom. VI, No. 17.

publicly and manifestly as such. This practically amounts to notoriety of fact, or at least a specific publicity and manifestation.[36]

Since the New Code does not specify the various delinquents to be refused ecclesiastical sepulture on these grounds, and since there is no innovation introduced in this detail—it is better to view this serious and risky matter in the light of the old law, where the public sinners are specifically designated. It is sufficient to mention only a few of these to avoid repetition of the delinquents already listed under the other captions. Usurers[37]—robbers[38]—violators of a church[39]—sorcerers and the like[40]—keepers of bagnios, and prostitutes.[41] In a class by themselves were listed those—of whom it was publicly known—who had neglected their Easter duty and who had died impenitent.[42] It may be well to remark here that this class of persons today cannot so easily be termed, "public and manifest sinners." Especially true is this in our larger cities where one knows so little of his neighbor's habits, traits or shortcomings. In fact, the Council of Quebec notes that the practise of the church demands that this penalty is not incurred "ipso facto" by neglect of the Easter duty, but requires the declaration of the Bishop. Consequently the pastor should notify the Ordinary of such a case and await his prudent judgment.[43] However, the case might yet occur and be truly evident. With due respect to the various necessary conditions and contingencies, the pastor should have proper respect for this penalty. The First Council of Baltimore issued a decree which demanded that the ecclesiastical rites be denied when Catholics were buried in Protestant or in civil (profane) cemeteries, in prefer-

---

36 Coronata, l. c., No. 263.

37 C. 3, XV, 19; Reiffenstuel, l. c., Tit. XXVIII, No. 82.

38 C. 2, XV, 17.

39 C. 2, XV, 26.

40 Inst. S. C. Prop. Fid., 6 Jun., 1817=Coll. P. F., No. 723.

41 Wernz, l. c., Tom. III, No. 781; Many, l. c., No. 220.

42 C. 12, XV, 33; Rom. Rit. Tit. II, C. 2, n. 6; Wernz, l. c., Nos. 740, 781.

43 Acta et Decreta, I Plen. Conc. Quebecensis, Tit. XIII, No. 605.

ence to nearby Catholic cemeteries.[44] The Second Plenary Council admitted that the rigor of this severe decree should be mitigated in many cases.[45] It was clearly perceived that, very often in the case of converts, their non-Catholic relatives would insist on such interment, and the pastor was directed to use his own judgment and celebrate the exsequies in the house, or even publicly in the church. Likewise in the case where Catholics could not obtain an exclusive right to a separate section in these civil cemeteries. The Third Plenary Council reaffirmed this mitigation in order to avoid distasteful conjecture and odium on the part of the non-Catholic relatives of the deceased, in these rather extreme cases. However, the Council warns the pastors that, except in these specified instances, he must obtain the express permission of the Ordinary before he may conduct the burial rites in a non-Catholic cemetery.[46]

The important feature to notice in dealing with all these cases, is that before the penalty of deprivation is to be applied, the fact that such a person was a public and manifest sinner must be clearly established.

CHAPTER III. IN CASE OF DOUBT

There may arise doubts as to the correct application of this penal law. The priest may be in doubt as to whether these serious delinquencies really have been committed—whether the person was guilty of the charge—whether he can be considered a public and manifest sinner—whether he died without exhibiting signs of repentance—and other less likely cases. The New Code prescribes in very clear terms what should be done in these doubtful matters.[1] If time allows one

---

44 Acta et Decreta, I Plen. Conc. Baltimorensis, l. c., No. 80.
45 Acta et Decreta, II Plen. Conc. Balt., l. c., Nos. 391, 392.
46 Acta et Decreta, III Plen. Conc. Balt., l. c., Nos. 317, 318.

---

1 Can. 1240, No. 2.

must consult the Ordinary and abide by his decision.[2] In the case of exempt Religious, the Ordinary is the Major Superior.[3] Having examined the case with its peculiar circumstances, and the doubt still remaining, then the body is to be allowed ecclesiastical sepulture. But if time did not permit of this consultation with the Ordinary, then the priest himself would decide for the sepulture, if the doubt was present. However, in following this procedure, one must take care that all scandal, or danger of, be removed when ecclesiastical sepulture is allowed in doubtful cases. This may be done in various ways by making known to the people the favorable circumstances in the case and the duty of charity towards the deceased. The Second Plenary Council of Baltimore prescribed—"In doubt, let the Ordinary be consulted if possible; otherwise however, let judgment lean to leniency and mercy. This, we especially counsel, whenever the deceased, having been overtaken by a sudden death, had no time for repentance: since, according to the norm of the law, 'odia restrindenda sunt.' "[4]

CHAPTER IV. EFFECT OF THIS DEPRIVATION

The New Code defines that the consequences of privation of ecclesiastical sepulture comprise—the denial of Requiem Mass, anniversaries and other public funeral services.[1]

1. The complete order of the funeral services and burial services, from the "levatio" to the burial in the sacred place, is withheld.[2]

---

2 S. C. S. Off., 6 Jul., 1898=Coll. P. F., No. 2007.
3 Can. 198, No. 2.
4 Acta et Decreta, l. c., No. 389.

---

1 Can. 1241.
2 S. C. S. Off., 13 Jan., 1818=Coll. P. F., No. 727; 7 Jul. 1864, Coll. P. F., No. 1257; S. C. Prop. Fid., 6 Jun., 1817=Coll. P. F., No. 723, n. 2; Rom. Rit. Tit. VI, C. 1, 2; Wernz, l. c., No. 780; Coronata, l. c., No. 266.

2. Consequently, the clergy may not officiate in any way.[3]

3. Note that this canon refers only to public services. Private Masses may be said for the repose of the soul of any of the persons mentioned in the foregoing canon, provided that there be no "communicatio in sacris."[4]

4. If it can be done without great inconvenience, the body of an "excommunicatus vitandus," who obtained interment in a sacred place contrary to the law, should be exhumed.[5] This canon requires close attention.

(1) Great inconvenience excuses from this extremity; i. e.—if the civil law forbade it.

(2) Only an "excommunicatus vitandus" is designated in this regulation. Such a one is he who has been excommunicated in name by the Holy See, the censure publicly announced, and an express declaration in the decree or sentence that he must be avoided.[6] One who lays violent hands on the person of the Roman Pontiff, becomes "ipso facto" "vitandus."[7] Exhumation is not prescribed for any other than an "excommunicatus vitandus."

(3) The permission of the Ordinary of the place is required before this exhumation take place.[8] Note that a Religious Superior cannot grant such permissiòn, since he is not an "Ordinary of the place."[9]

(4) Then, the body is to be interred in that lot especially assigned for this purpose.[10]

(5) What practical import has this regulation? The civil governments and municipalities in so many places do not allow the church her rights and privileges in these matters, and present obstacles to the carrying out of this prescription and thus provide this "grave incom-

---

3 Many, l. c., No. 222.

4 S. C. S. Off., 14 Feb., 1827; Coll. P. F., No. 793; S. C. S. Off., 27 Jul., 1892; Coll. P. F., No. 1808, n. II.

5 Can. 1242.

6 Can. 2258, No. 2.

7 Can. 2343, No. 1, 1'.

8 Can. 1214, No. 1; Rit. Rom. Tit. VI, C. 1, n. 15.

9 Can. 198, No. 2.

10 Can. 1212=See Section I, page .

modum." Seldom will anyone be in a position to be able to apply this law of the church.

CHAPTER V. IN CASE OF SERIOUS CONSEQUENCES

It may happen, that in a peculiar case, the denial of ecclesiastical sepulture would involve serious issues. A grave "damnum" may threaten the priest who refuses the rites. A serious dissension may arise among the people. Law suits, contention and strife may result. In such distress prudent judgment would determine that the penalty had better not be enforced. Of course, religion must not be brought into contempt in any way, from this procedure, and all danger of scandal be dispelled. This privation of ecclesiastical sepulture is an ecclesiastical law, which, generally speaking does not bind "gravi incommodo." The church must not suffer in any way, from the infliction of any of her penalties.[1]

CHAPTER VI. PENALTIES FOR THE BREAKING OF THIS LAW

The church refuses ecclesiastical sepulture, to several classes of persons: some are to be excluded under pain of sin only—others under pain of censure also. The New Code contains two penalties for certain persons who disregard this law of the denial of ecclesiastical sepulture to the specified unworthy.

---

1 S. C. S. Off., 19 Sep., 1877=Coll. P. F., No. 1483; S. C. S. Off., 15 Dec., 1886=Coll. P. F., No. 1665; S. C. S. Off., 6 Jul., 1898=Coll. P. F., No. 2007; D'Annibale, Lib. I, No. 114; Wernz, l. c., No. 782; Ojetti, l. c., "Sepult.," No. 3704.

1. Excommunication

An excommunication "latae sententiae" reserved to no one, is incurred by those who dare to command or compel the granting of ecclesiastical sepulture to infidels, apostates, heretics, or schismatics and "excommunicati" or "interdicti" after a declaratory or condemnatory sentence.[1]

(1) The meaning and force of this canon is apparent; little discussion is necessary. Always to be kept in mind are those adjuncts circumstances and conditions essential to the law of deprivation. These have already been treated to some extent in the foregoing pages and require no further discussion here.

(2) The present law exhibits a mitigation of the former severity. In the Constitution of Pius IX "Apost. Sed." is provided that an excommunication "latae sententiae" reserved to no one, is incurred by those who command or compel the granting of ecclesiastical sepulture to notorious heretics or those excommunicated or interdicted in name.[2] The difference and lesion are at once apparent. The old law made no mention of "ausus fuerit"—the New Code requires that this condition of "daring" be present. Ignorance of the fact or law, as long as it was not affected ignorance, would then excuse from the penalty.[3] Likewise the various causes diminishing imputability enjoy their vigor.[4]

(3) However, in some respects the New Code is more severe, inasmuch as it extends the class of unworthy persons. Infidels, apostates and schismatics were not comprised in the Constitution "Apostolicae Sedis."

(4) The excommunicated and interdicted persons comprised, are only those censured after a condemnatory or declaratory sentence, whether they are "vitandi" or

1 Can. 2339.
2 12 Oct., 1869, IV, n. 1=Coll. P. F. No. 1348.
3 Can. 2229; Sole, l. c., No. 367.
4 Sole, l. c., No. 367.

"tolerati."[5] The heretics and schismatics must be notoriously attached to some sect.[6]

(5) "Mandare," refers to the prescribing, ordering, commanding or demanding of a definite action; and generally applies to a person of some public authority.[7] "Cogere," refers to compulsion by applying force or causing grave fear. Consequently, mere enticement, bribing, and the like, would not bring about this censure.[8]

(6) Note that the list of unworthy persons contained in this Canon 2339 is not the same as the complete list of Canon 1240, No. 1. Apply this penal law only in these specified cases.[9]

(7) The censure is incurred only when the effect follows.[10]

(8) Some authors would have it that this law refers only to the interment in a sacred place.[11] But why this restriction of the term, ecclesiastical sepulture, to mean only burial? The New Code has explicitly stated that ecclesiastical sepulture consists in the three-fold service, transferring the body to the church—holding the funeral services there—and committing the body to interment in the cemetery.[12] Other authors maintain that the Code continues this significance in using these terms in reference to the denial of the rites. This latter opinion certainly appears to be a more tenable and consistent interpretation.[13]

3. Interdict

An interdict from entering the church, reserved to the Ordinary, is incurred by those who, of their own accord, freely grant ecclesiastical sepulture to those specified unworthy persons.[14]

---

5 Cans. 1240, No. 1, 2'; 2258, 2259.
6 Can. 1240, No. 1, 1'.
7 Sole, l. c., No. 367; Cavigliolі, l. c., No. 171; Coronata, l. c., No. 267.
8 Sole, l. c., No. 367.
9 Can. 2339.
10 D'Annibale, l. c., No. 167; Sole, l. c., No. 367; Cavigliolі, l. c., No. 171; Coronata, l. c., No. 267.
11 Cavigliolі, C. No. 170; Capello, l. c., No. 137; Chelodi, No. 73.
12 Can. 1204.
13 Sole, l. c., No. 367; Coronata, l. c., No. 267.
14 Can. 2339.

(1) The Constitution, "Apost. Sed." is practically identical.[15]

(2) The use of the term, "sponte" implies that fear or force would excuse from this censure.[16]

(3) Since, only clerics can grant ecclesiastical sepulture, it is clear that only those clerics who have such authority would be subject to this interdict.[17]

(4) By this interdict, the censured parties are forbidden to celebrate the divine offices, to preach, or to conduct funeral services. If they merely assist at these functions, it would not be necessary to exclude them.[18] Ecclesiastical sepulture would be denied them if the interdict was accompanied by a condemnatory or declaratory sentence.[19]

CONCLUSION

In concluding, it is well to call to mind that benevolent instruction of the S. Congregation of the Holy Office, of almost a century ago, concerning this drastic procedure of the deprivation of ecclesiastical sepulture. "Holy Mother Church, ever benign and compassionate towards her children, ardently desires that they be saved. Imbued with this spirit, His eminence, the Cardinal knows well that the wickedness of the impious will not reflect on whatever day one is converted from his evil way."[1] Such is the mind of the church. The penal law is strict: the earthly resting place of the faithful departed must not suffer any profanation. Yet, the conditions necessary, demand this infliction only in those clearly defined cases of guilt: while charity and prudence should guide the pastor in every emergency.

---

15 12 Oct., 1869, No. VI=Coll. P. F., No. 3348.

16 Sole, l. c., No. 368.

17 D'Annibale, l. c., No. 220; Many, l. c., No. 224; Sole, l. c., No. 367.

18 Can. 2277; Sole, No. 246=Cavigliola, l. c., No. 182; Coronata, l. c., No. 267.

19 Cans. 1240, No. 1, 2'; 1242; Coronata, l. c., No. 267.

BIBLIOGRAPHY

Sources

Codex Juris Canonici. Rome, 1917.

Acta Apostolicae Sedis (1909-1922). Rome.

Acta Sanctae Sedis (1865-1906). Rome.

Corpus Juris Canonici (Richter). Leipsig, 1839.

Sacrosancta Concilia (Labbeus-Cossartius). Paris, 1671.

Canones et Decreta, Concilii Tridentini. Rome, 1913.

Decreta Authentica Congreg. S. Rituum. Rome, 1898-1900.

Collectanea S. Cong. de Prop. Fid. Rome, 1917.

Missale Romanum. Ratisbon, 1920.

Rituale Romanum. Rome, 1913.

Pontificale Romanum. Milan, 1855.

II Plen. Conc. Baltimorensis (1866). Baltimore, 1868.

III Plen. Conc. Baltimorensis (1884). Baltimore, 1886.

Acta et Decreta, Conc. Plen. Quebecensis Primi. (1909). Quebec, 1912.

Authors

Aichner, S.—Compendium Juris Ecclesiastici. Brixinae, 1887.

American Ecclesiastical Review. Philadelphia.

Augustine, P. C.—Commentary on Canon Law. St. Louis, 1921.

Bargilliat, J.—Praelectiones Juris Canonici. Paris, 1921.

Ayrinhac, H. A.—Penal Legislation in the New Code. New York, 1920.

Blat, A.—Comment. Textus Codicis Juris Canonici. Rome, 1920-1923.

Bingham, Jos.—Antiquities. Oxford, 1855.

Catholic Encyclopedia. New York.

Capello, F.—De Censuris. Turin, 1919.
Cavagnis, Card. F.—Institutiones Juris Publici Eccles. Rome, 1855.
Cavigioli, J.—Censurae Latae Sententiae. Turin, 1919.
Chelodi, J.—Jus Poenale. Trentino, 1920.
Creusen, J.—Tabulae Fontium Christianae. Freiburg, 1921.
D'Angelo, Don Sosio.—Della Sepoltura Ecclesiastica. Rome, 1913.
D'Annibale, Card.—Summae Theologiae Moralis. Rome, 1891.
De Angelis, P.—Praelectiones Juris Canonici. Rome, 1908.
Denzinger-Bannwart.—Enchiridion Symb. et Definit. Freiburg, 1921.
Devoti, J.—Institutiones Canonicarum. Leodicii, 1860.
Duchesne, L.—Origines de Culte Chretien. Paris, 1889.
Ferraris, F. L.—Bibliotheca Canonica, etc. Rome, 1885.
Gasparri, Card.—De Ssma. Eucharistia. Paris, 1897.
Irish Ecclesiastical Record. Dublin.
Lanciani—Christian and Pagan Rome. London, 1892.
Laurentius, J.—Institutiones Juris Ecclesiastici. Freiburg, 1914.
Leclercq, Dom. H.—Manuel D'Archeologie Chretienne. Paris, 1907.
Lehmkuhl, A.—Theologia Moralis. Freiburg, 1910.
Lehmkuhl, A.—Quaestiones Praecipuae Morales. Freiburg, 1918.
Many, S.—Praelectiones de Locis Sacris. Paris, 1904.
Maroto, R.—Institutiones Juris Canonici. Rome, 1921.
Moulart, F. J.—De Sepultura et Coemeteriis. Louvain, 1862.
Murphy, J.—Parish Priests and Christian Burial. Philadelphia, 1922.
Noldin, H.—Summa Theologiae Moralis. Ratisbon, 1921.

Northcote, J. S.—The Roman Catacombs. London, 1891.

Ojetti, B.—Synopsis Rerum Moral. et Juris Pontif. Rome, 1909.

Phillips, G.—Compendium Juris Ecclesiastici. Ratisbon, 1875.

Reiffenstuel, P. A.—Jus Canonicum Universum. Venetiis, 1726.

Sanguineti, S.—Juris Ecclesiastici Institutiones. Rome, 1896.

Schmalzgrueber—Jus Ecclesiasticum Universum. Rome, 1845.

Smith, S. B.—Elements of Ecclesiastical Law. New York, 1881.

Sole, J.—De Delictis et Poenis. Rome, 1920.

Summa Divi Thomae Aquinatis. Rome, 1894.

Tanquerey, A.—Synopsis Theologiae Dogmaticae. New York, 1913.

Thomassinus—Vetus et Nova Ecclesiae Disciplina. Magontiaci, 1787.

Vermeersch, A.—Summa Juris Canonici. Bruges, 1921.

Vermeersch—Creusen, Epitome Juris Canonici. Bruges, 1921.

Wernz, F.—Jus Decretalium. Prati, 1911-1914.

Universitas Catholica Americae

Washington, D. C.

Sacra Facultas Theologica

1922-1923

No. 18

CANONES

DEUS LUX MEA

CANONES

QUOS

AD DOCTORATUS GRADUM

IN

IURE CANONICO

Apud Universitatem Catholicam Americae

CONSEQUENDUM

PUBLICE PROPUGNABIT

IOANNES ANTONIUS O'REILLY

Sacerdos Archidioecesis Ottaviensis

JURIS CANONICI LICENTIATUS

HORA XI A. M., DIE XXIX MAII, A. D. MCMXXIII

I.	De ambitu. Codicis.	(Cans. 1-7)
II.	De legibus ecclesiasticis.	(Cans. 8-13)
III.	De consuetudine.	(Cans. 25-30)
IV.	De temporis supputatione.	(Cans. 31-35)
V.	De cessatione privilegiorum.	(Cans. 72-78)
VI.	De dispensationibus.	(Cans. 80-86)
VII.	De personis.	(Cans. 87-89)
VIII.	De domicilio.	(Cans. 90-95)
IX.	De obligationibus clericorum.	(Cans. 124-128)
X.	De Romano Pontifice.	(Cans. 218-221)
XI.	De Episcopis.	(Cans. 329-333)
XII.	De consultoribus dioecesanis.	(Cans. 423-428)
XIII.	De officiis parochorum.	(Cans. 464-470)
XIV.	De vicariis paroecialibus.	(Cans. 471-478)
XV.	De Religiosis.	(Cans. 487-491)
XVI.	De tertiis ordinibus saecularibus.	(Cans. 702-706)
XVII.	De ministro Baptismi.	(Cans. 738-744)
XVIII.	De iis qui possunt esse patrini.	(Cans. 765-766)
XIX.	De ministro Confirmationis.	(Cans. 782-785)
XX.	De subiecto Confirmationis.	(Cans. 786-789)
XXI.	De ministro Sacrae Communionis.	(Cans. 845-852)
XXII.	De tempore et loco quo Sacra Communio distribui possit.	(Cans. 867-869)
XXIII.	De loco ad confessiones excipiendas.	(Cans. 908-910)
XXIV.	De irregularitatibus in Sacris Ordinibus.	(Cans. 983-986)
XXV.	De tempore et loco sacrae ordinationis.	(Cans. 1006-1009)
XXVI.	De notione Matrimonii.	(Cans. 1012-1018)

XXVII.	De publicatione bannorum.	(Cans. 1022-1026)
XXVIII.	De impedimentis in genere.	(Cans. 1035-1042)
XXIX.	De impedimento mixtae religionis.	(Cans. 1060-1064)
XXX.	De impedimentis Ordinis Sacrae et Professionis Religiosae.	(Cans. 1072-1073)
XXXI.	De impedimentis consanguinitatis et affinitatis.	(Cans. 1076-1077)
XXXII.	De Matrimonio conscientiae.	(Cans. 1104-1107)
XXXIII.	De tempore et loco celebrationis Matrimonii.	(Cans. 1108-1109)
XXXIV.	De dedicatione locae sacrae.	(Cans. 1154-1160)
XXXV.	De aedificatione ecclesiae.	(Cans. 1161-1164)
XXXVI.	De violatione et reconciliatione ecclesiae.	(Cans. 1172-1177)
XXXVII.	De coemeteriis.	(Cans. 1205-1214)
XXXVIII.	De ecclesia funerante, ex iure commune.	(Cans. 1215-1218)
XXXIX.	De ecclesia funerante, ex iure speciali.	(Cans. 1219-1221)
XL.	De iure electionis.	(Cans. 1223-1227)
XLI.	De portione paroeciali.	(Cans. 1236-1238)
XLII.	De iis quibus sepultura ecclesiastica concedenda est aut neganda.	(Cans. 1239-1242)
XLIII.	De catechetica institutione.	(Cans. 1329-1336)
XLIV.	De tribunalibus.	(Cans. 1569-1571)
XLV.	De Notario, Promotore iustitiae, vinculi Defensore.	(Cans. 1585-1590)
XLVI.	De tribunali ordinario secundae instantiae.	(Cans. 1594-1596)
XLVII.	De foro competenti in causis matrimonialibus.	(Cans. 1960-1965)
XLVIII.	De appelationibus in causis matrimonialibus.	(Cans. 1986-1989)

XLIX.	De causis contra sacram ordinationem.	(Cans. 1993-1998)
L.	De modo procedendi in remotione parochorum amovibilium.	(Cans. 2157-2161)
LI.	De modo procedendi in translatione parochorum.	(Cans. 2162-2167)
LII.	De natura delicti eiusque divisione.	(Cans. 2195-2198)
LIII.	De conatu delicti.	(Cans. 2212-2213)
LIV.	De superiore potestatem coactivam habente.	(Cans. 2220-2225)
LV.	De iis quae excusant a poenis vel non.	(Can. 2229)
LVI.	De notione censurae.	(Cans. 2241-2242)
LVII.	De absolutione censurae in casibus urgentioribus.	(Can. 2254)
LVIII.	De notione excommunicationis.	(Cans. 2257-2259)
LIX.	De interdicto locali.	(Cans. 2269-2274)
LX.	De variis suspensionibus.	(Can. 2279)

* * * * * *

Vidit Sacra Facultas:

CAROLUS F. AIKEN, S. T. D., p. t. Decanus.

HENRICUS SCHUMACHER, S. T. D., p. t. a Secretis.

Vidit Rector Universitatis:

†THOMAS J. SHAHAN, S. T. D.

LIFE

John Anthony O'Reilly was born in Perth, Ontario, August 22, 1899. He received his elementary and secondary education at the Separate Schools of the City of Ottawa, Ont., and at the University of Ottawa. On September 14, 1915, he entered St. Augustine's Seminary, Toronto, Ont., and was ordained to the priesthood April 17, 1922. He entered the Catholic University of America, Washington, D. C., September 27, 1921, and attended the lectures of the Monsignor Filippo Bernardini, in Canon Law, of Rev. Dr. John A. Ryan, in Moral Theology, of Rev. Dr. Roderick MacEachen, in Educational Religion.

To his professors and instructors, and to the revisers of his manuscript, he extends his grateful appreciation for their services in his behalf.

www.ingramcontent.com/pod-product-compliance
Lightning Source LLC
LaVergne TN
LVHW050206080826
844660LV00012B/367

* 9 7 8 0 8 1 3 2 2 2 0 9 7 *